LIFE TOUCHED WITH WONDER

LIFE TOUCHED WITH WONDER

WINDOWS
of HOPE

FROM THE EDITORS OF READER'S DIGEST

THE READER'S DIGEST ASSOCIATION, INC.
PLEASANTVILLE, NEW YORK

ISBN 0-7621-8852-9

Printed in the United States of America

Book design by Patrice Sheridan

You can also visit us on the World Wide Web at http://www.readersdigest.com

CONTENTS

LIFE TOUCHED
WITH WONDER

Men wonder at the height of mountains, the huge waves of the sea, the broad flow of rivers, the course of the stars—and forget to wonder at themselves.
— *St. Augustine*

We feel awe when we see a grand landscape or view the majesty of a starry sky. But there's also wonder in a child's kiss when you're feeling down, in a friend's unexpected recovery from a frightening illness, in a walk on a hushed, snowy night. Such moments take us by surprise and lift us from the mundane and the familiar. Suddenly, inexplicably, we catch a glimpse of a reality beyond ourselves, and see evidence that there is something beautiful, merciful, loving knit into the fabric of creation — even in ourselves.

In fact, ordinary people can be the most gifted messengers of wonder. Their stories offer compelling evidence of the power of the spirit in daily life. In this new book series we have selected the best of such true-life stories and present them in separate volumes organized around themes, including hope, love, courage and healing.

Windows of Hope will introduce you to people with troubles and concerns common to us all. You will not only be moved by these stories, you will find a bright beacon of hope to help guide your own journey as well.

"SOLD! TO THE YOUNG MAN IN SHORTS"

BY

PAUL HARVEY

You'd be amazed at the stuff that turns up in a police department property room. Police recover things, then nobody claims them. Or evidence is held and released. All sorts of things. Cameras and stereo speakers, TV sets and tools and tool boxes and car radios. And once a year these unclaimed items are sold at auction. This year at the police auction in Kansas City, Mo., there was a large number of bicycles.

When the very first bicycle came up and the auctioneer asked who'd start the bidding, a youngster right down in front said, "Five dollars." Tiny youngster—ten—maybe 12.

"I've got five, will you give me ten? Ten, who'll bid 15?"

As the bidding continued the auctioneer looked back at the young man down front. The boy did not respond.

Later another bicycle came up, and again the boy bid $5 but would go no higher. This went on through several bicycles. Each time the boy bid $5; never more. And $5 was not nearly enough. The bikes were selling for $35 or $40, and some even for more than $100.

During a brief intermission, the auctioneer asked the boy why he had let some of those good bikes sell without bidding higher. The young man explained that $5 was all he had.

Back to the auction: there were cameras and CB radios still to be sold, and some more bicycles. On each bicycle, the boy bid $5. And on each, someone else bid much more.

But now the assembled crowd is beginning to notice the boy who always opens the bidding. The crowd is beginning to recognize what is happening.

After a tedious hour and a half, the auction is beginning to wind down. But there is still one bicycle left, and it is a dandy. A shiny, like-new ten-speed with 27-inch wheels, dual-position brake levers, stem shifters and a generator light set.

The auctioneer asks, "Do I hear a bid?"

And the young man near the front—who by now has all but given up— quietly repeats: "Five dollars."

And the auctioneer stops his chant. Just stops. Stands there.

And the audience sits silent. Not one hand is raised. Not one voice calls out a second bid.

Until the auctioneer says: "SOLD! To the young man in the shorts and sneakers—for $5!"

And the audience applauds.

And a small boy's face lights up like one of the most beautiful sights you ever saw, as he trades the $5 scrunched up in his sweaty fist for what is surely the most beautiful bicycle in the world.

ALL GOD'S ANGELS

BY

PAT LANGFORD

*D*eep in the Nebraska winter, some years ago, I felt our family had reached a pinnacle of happiness. Thanks to my husband Ken's hard work, I was able to stay home with our three blond, blue-eyed daughters, Lezlie, 14, Lynn, ten, and Lesa Marie, six, savoring their energy, their loving good cheer — and the delightful differences between them. Indeed, what parents have not talked quietly in the night, after the children are asleep, of the unfathomable mystery of God's hand in the creation of their offspring?

Of our girls, Lesa Marie, our youngest, was known throughout our neighborhood in North Platte as smart, funny and breathtakingly free-spirited, always dancing to her own music. She was constantly in motion.

Jumping from bed each morning, she raced to her sisters' rooms, laughing uproariously as she teased them awake. She delighted in stuffing their belongings down the laundry chute: teddy bears, hairbrushes, shoes — even our cat, Spook, made several yowling trips to the laundry room.

Among Lesa's chores was to empty the upstairs wastebaskets into the kitchen trash. It occurred to me one day that I had not seen her doing this — yet the baskets were empty. Scouting around, I found all the trash in the heat registers! Lesa explained this was faster than taking it downstairs.

To embarrass her older and more dignified sisters, Lesa would drag our milk box into the front yard and climb up on it, facing the street. Using the garden-hose nozzle as a microphone, she would belt out "Bad, Bad Leroy Brown," emphasizing "baddest man in the whole *damned* town." She knew she would have to contribute to the family's "language bank," which we paid for using "unbecoming" language. The accumulated money went into the collection plate at church. To Lesa, this was an opportunity: complete freedom of expression for only a nickel.

Neighbors seemed charmed to have this blond dynamo pop in. "She flits around like a pretty little butterfly," one said.

Lesa was particularly inclined to visit when she was in the doghouse at home. An older couple once told me that, upon taking a seat, Lesa heaved a dramatic sigh and complained, "That woman over there is working me to death!" That woman, of course, was her mother, and I was probably sorting the trash out of the registers.

On a cold spring day in 1973, Lesa walked home after kindergarten dragging a stick. "I bet you didn't know it was Arbor Day," she said. "They gave everybody a tree. This will be beautiful when it grows up."

The "tree" was a two-foot stick showing no sign of life. The wrapping on its bulb had been dragged off, and the exposed hint of roots looked dry and hopeless. But Lesa cajoled Ken into helping her plant the stick in the back yard. "I'm naming her Angela," she announced, "because it's going to take all God's angels to make her grow."

Every day, Lesa watered Angela, patting and earnestly speaking to it, then bowing her head and saying a blessing. Her faith was perfect that she would nurture this stick into its full magnificence as a tree.

One summer morning, Lesa burst into the kitchen. "Two leaves, Mom!" she shouted. "Two leaves!" Indeed, the stick named Angela had produced a pair of tiny green leaves. Lesa called it our Hallelujah Day.

Soon, Angela became part of the family. We began to humor Lesa

 by speaking to the tree. Once, when Lezlie brushed the lawn mower against Angela, Lesa demanded that Lezlie apologize. Lezlie bent over Angela, saying politely, "I'm so sorry I bumped you. I promise I won't do it again." By summer's end I found myself silently acknowledging Angela's presence even when Lesa wasn't around.

That winter of 1973-74, undaunted by snow, Lesa regularly went out to encourage Angela to sleep well and get ready to wake up in the spring. Summer brought new leaves — and celebration over Angela's grand achievement. As we shared Lesa's joy, she stood with a hand on Angela, smiling impishly at the rest of us.

That is the picture of our youngest I will hold always, shimmering in the sunshine of my mind's eye.

In August 1974, two days before Lesa's seventh birthday, around noon, a surgeon suddenly filled the doorway of the Omaha hospital room where Ken and I waited. Since dawn, he had been operating on Lesa's chest. "I don't need to look in a microscope to tell you this is the most malignant tumor I've ever seen," he said grimly, leaving us in shock. We never saw or heard from him again.

Two weeks earlier, Lesa had awakened me one night. "Mom, I feel all hot inside," she said. Soon she developed a severe cough. A week later, I noticed a swelling on her chest. X rays showed a growth. Within hours, Lesa, Ken and I had set out on the five-hour drive to Omaha.

There the days ran together in a mind-numbing labyrinth of doctors, tests, conflicting advice and torturous decisions. Then came the surgery and devastating diagnosis: non-Hodgkin's lymphoblastic lymphoma. To subdue this monster that raged within our daughter's chest, we followed the twin sirens of radiation and chemotherapy. Nothing was more horrible than to hear our precious daughter's cries of anguish during some of the procedures. The treatments shrank the tumor, but it returned with a vengeance.

Despite the hundreds of times in my life I've said the Twenty-Third Psalm, I cannot pretend I was comforted as I walked that dark valley. Early on, I dreamed Lesa was dead, and though I never told Ken, I was certain this would be the outcome.

During that last wonderful Christmas before the disease struck, Santa had left Lesa a huge stuffed dog with floppy ears named Norman. Lesa took "Normie" to The Children's Hospital of Denver when she went to undergo five weeks of radiation. Each day, she lay alone in that barren room to be "zapped," as she put it. I stood at the window, holding Norman.

Back home and on chemotherapy, Lesa spent most of her time in her room. When she reacted violently to the chemo, she hugged Norman for comfort. Buttons, our little schnauzer, kept her company too. Dr. Lewis Harden, a compassionate young pediatrician, came night or day as Lesa needed him.

Often Lesa and I talked for long hours into the night. I sensed at times that she wanted to ask me things about her illness — to ask whether she was going to die. But she never did, and I did not know how to help her ask. Nor would I have known what to say if she had asked. So I said nothing.

I remember the morning that Lesa's soft blond hair began to come out in clumps as I brushed it. Although it seared me to the core, I tried to muster my calm and said to Lesa, "Why don't we go ahead and brush all of this out?" At just that moment, Lezlie appeared in the doorway. I looked up at her pretty, gentle face. "Here, Mom," Lezlie said calmly. "Let me do that for you."

Many years went by before Lezlie and I ever spoke of that moment — only to discover that it had been of wrenching importance to us both. For her, it was the single time throughout the ordeal that she had an opportunity to give something of herself. She, like the rest of us, was determined to pretend, no matter what, that life was normal.

By June 1975, Lesa had rallied a bit and was even riding her bicycle. But soon a relapse forced a return to Denver. Nothing more could be done, doctors said, to treat the cancer effectively, and it would not be fair to put her through more chemotherapy. With Lesa hanging on to Norman, we drove home.

Even though we never gave Lesa any verbal indication that she was dying, I am convinced she knew. In spite of this, her good cheer never failed. Nor did she ever admit to being frightened.

Privately I decided to help Lesa live as fully as she could until her time came. She was determined to take swimming lessons — and she did. She and Norman went visiting. A neighbor recruited her to help plan a surprise party for his wife. The whole neighborhood came. Lesa was thrilled.

Two weeks later, on the hot afternoon of August 17, with Norman beside her, our little girl lapsed into a peaceful coma. Her breathing slowed and finally seemed to stop. For a long time, Dr. Harden listened for the next heartbeat. At last, I broke the silence.

"Is it over?"

"Yes," he said softly. "It is over."

At Lesa's funeral, the church was filled. Draped near the altar was a banner with the figure of a whimsically floating butterfly. Incredibly, we, her family, were so determined to "be strong" that not one of us shed a tear.

Then we all went home to our quiet house. Upstairs, Norman sat alone on Lesa's bed. Outside in the hot sun, Angela stood alone. Inside our hearts we, too, were alone.

I had assumed that Lesa's death would bring our family a release. As Christians we believed that once Lesa's suffering had vanished and she was with God, we would embrace and resume our fruitful lives.

That did not happen.

Our way of "being strong" and "getting on with life" was to sell Lesa's furniture and donate her toys and clothes to charity, although some instinct moved me to stash Norman quietly in a closet. Within days, the only visible reminder of Lesa in the house was Buttons, who spent hours plastered against the floor in Lesa's room, eyes sad. She was the only one able to be open about her loss.

Let no one despair, even though in the darkest night the last star of hope may disappear.

FRIEDRICH SCHILLER

The rest of us avoided the subject. Now that Lesa was gone, we seemed to find it easier not to speak of her at all. Indeed, it was as though each of us were in a glass cube. We could see and hear one another, but we could not touch each other with our thoughts.

Alone, I had to face the fear that in my efforts to shield Lesa from her illness, I had actually isolated her — stranding her in fear and uncertainty. I did not know what would bring about my healing. I was sure, though, that it was important to remain strong — not to cry.

During these dark times, our main link to Lesa was the tree Angela, now seven feet tall. But our home was all too reminiscent of Lesa's dying. We agreed to move immediately to another house, solemnly promising to fetch Angela in the spring.

In hindsight, our flight from ourselves seems so pitiful. When we moved into our new house, I knew instantly that we had brought all of our agony with us.

On a cold morning in April, we went back for Angela. We felt a powerful if unspoken obligation to take care of her as Lesa would have done. We planted Angela in our new back yard, where we could see her from the family room.

Life, of course, went on. Ken threw himself into his work as a banker; I spent my time helping Lynn and Lezlie grow up. Taking care of Angela — who responded with magnificent good health — was our only way of continuing silently to remember Lesa.

Seven years after Lesa's death, Ken asked me to go with him to a gathering of bereaved parents called The Compassionate Friends, as a favor to a friend starting a chapter.

At the meeting, a moderator told the group that, having lost a child, we all were uniquely qualified to help others cope with the same loss. I found myself getting angry. Suddenly I blurted out, "Why the hell would I want to help someone else? No one ever helped me!"

I sat back, astonished at myself. Everyone looked at me in silence. I was glad when I could slink home.

Then another thing happened. Lezlie, out of college and living in Omaha, called. Something had gone wrong that seemed overwhelming. She was upset, and in the middle of explaining it all, she suddenly delivered these amazing words:

"Mom, where is Norman? Didn't you keep him? Please go get him and give him a big hug for me." When I asked why, she said, "I just need to touch base with Lesa."

There on the phone, the emotional floodgates opened. We began to talk about what a funny and wise and wonderful child Lesa had been. Thanks to big, floppy-eared Norman, my daughter and I had begun exchanging our deepest feelings.

On that day, Norman emerged from the closet and became a prominent part of our household. My life began to change as I started telling others about the joy and the lessons in Lesa's short life.

As I became comfortable sharing my pain with others in The Compassionate Friends, I reached a powerful realization. In my misery, I had been waiting for someone to help me. I now saw that my healing lay in helping others. I earned a master's degree in counseling and co-founded a mental-health service. My specialty is helping those who have lost loved ones.

Each Christmas now, I meet with families who have lost a child. Beside me is Norman, shaggy with age, but reflecting still the adoration heaped upon him by Lesa. I tell the group how for years Norman was wrapped in plastic in the closet — put there to subdue memories of Lesa. I tell them about my family's long struggle to face its grief. I encourage them to resist the urge to "be strong" — and to embrace the memories of their child who has died and each other. Only then, I say, can the child come alive in their hearts, as Lesa has for me — alive to be with them always.

Lynn, who was 12 when Lesa died, never spoke of her sister in the early years. She thought The Compassionate Friends was "silly." Then one night while in college and taking a course on death and dying, she made an emotional phone call like the one I received years earlier from Lezlie. Today, Lynn, too, enjoys sharing her memories of Lesa.

With our daughters married, Ken and I moved to a smaller place in 1988. This time, our beloved Angela was too big to move. As a gift to Ken, I had a photograph made of her in full bloom; it hangs in our bedroom.

In late 1990, when Lesa would have been 23, Ken used money that would have gone for her education to establish college scholarships for needy students.

I am happy today — satisfied that my long trek through the valley of the shadow is over. Goodness and mercy have restored my soul. I know that hope can be found in tragedy and that promise abounds in every life, no matter how short. I know, too, that the key to my recovery came when I opened my heart to allow the blessings of Lesa's memory to blossom — and when I began to fill the void of her loss by giving of myself to others in need.

Lesa's greatest legacy to us is Angela. Now a lush green hackberry at least 30 feet tall, it stands as eloquent testimony to a child's faith. Lesa never doubted that the hopeless little stick would grow into a magnificent tree. While we were supposed to be Lesa's teachers, in reality she was the one teaching us — about faith and love, and the towering power of all God's angels.

If you do not hope, you will not
find what is beyond your hopes.

ST. CLEMENT OF ALEXANDRIA

MONDAY MORNING MIRACLE

BY
PATTIE WIGAND,
AS TOLD TO PHILIP YANCEY

The sun is shining when I get on the southbound No. 151 bus. But Chicago's winter landscape is at its dingiest —leafless trees, mounds of slush, cars splattered with salt.

The bus cruises through scenic Lincoln Park for a few miles, but no one looks out the windows. We passengers sit jammed together in heavy clothes, lulled by the monotonous grind of the motor and the stuffy, overheated air.

No one speaks. That's one of the unwritten rules of Chicago commuting. Although we see the same faces every day, we prefer to hide behind our newspapers. The symbolism is striking: people who sit so close together are using those thin sheets of newsprint to keep their distance.

As the bus approaches the Magnificent Mile, a row of glittering skyscrapers along Michigan Avenue, a voice suddenly rings out: "Attention! Attention!"

Papers rattle. Necks crane.

"This is your driver speaking."

Stillness. We look at the back of the driver's head. His voice has authority.

"Put your papers down. All of you."

The papers come down, an inch at a time. The driver waits. The papers are folded and placed on our laps.

"Now, turn and face the person next to you. Go ahead."

Amazingly, we all do it. Still, no one smiles. Just mindless obedience, the herd instinct at work.

I face an older woman, her head wrapped tightly in a red scarf. I see her nearly every day. Our eyes meet. We wait, unblinking, for the next order from the driver.

"Now, repeat after me. . . ." It is a command, delivered in the tones of a drill sergeant. "Good morning, neighbor!"

Our voices are weak, timid. For many of us, these are the first words we have spoken today. But we say them in unison, like schoolchildren, to the stranger beside us.

We smile reflexively. We cannot help it. There is the feeling of relief, that we are not being kidnapped or robbed. But more, there is the faint sense of unleashing a common civility long repressed. We have said it; the barrier has been broken. *Good morning, neighbor.* It was not so hard after all. Some of us repeat it. Others shake hands. Many laugh.

The bus driver says nothing more. He doesn't need to. Not a single newspaper goes back up. The bus hums with conversation. We start by shaking our heads over this crazy driver, which leads to other commuting stories.

I hear laughter, a warm, bubbly sound I have never heard before on bus No. 151.

When we reach my stop, I say good-by to my seatmate, then jump from the doorstep to avoid a puddle. Four other buses have pulled up

at the same stop, disgorging passengers. The riders still seated inside look like statues —unmoving, silent. Except for those on my bus. As No. 151 drives away, I smile as I watch the animated faces of the passengers. This day is starting off better than most.

I look back at the driver. He is studying his mirror, searching for an opening in the traffic. He gives no sign of being aware that he's just pulled off a Monday morning miracle.

Hope smiles on the threshold of the year to
come, whispering that it will be happier.

ALFRED LORD TENNYSON

ROOM AT THE TABLE

BY

JAMES DIBELLO

In our intensely Catholic home in Indiana, angels were members of the family. My Italian grandmother always set an extra place for our guardian angel on feast days. On our birthdays, we six children set the place ourselves. Grandma said it was a way to thank the angel and to ask for help in the coming year.

I mean we *really* believed in angels. In school the nuns taught us about them. At Mass, we let our guardian angel into the pew first. One of the earliest prayers I learned was "Angel of God, my guardian dear, to whom God's love entrusts me here, ever this day be at my side, to lead and guard, to light and guide, Amen."

Otherwise, my childhood was ordinary until I was 14. That year, my favorite brother, Frank, who was eight, began to tire and bruise easily. To cheer him up, I taught him how to ride my bike. Before long, though, he couldn't even push the pedals and was in the hospital more often than not. I didn't know it at the time, but he had leukemia.

One day my parents came home from the hospital crying. The parish priest who was with them told us that Frank's angel had taken him to heaven. I was so sick at heart that I just cried and cried. Our grandmother was so distraught that she forgot her English and reverted to Italian.

As soon as I dried my tears, a terrible anger began to grow in me like a piece of metal turning red, orange, yellow and finally white hot. *Why didn't my parents tell me Frank was going to die?* I silently screamed. *And how could his angel have allowed it?* I hated Frank's angel. What a stupid thing to believe in.

My anger didn't go away. That summer, I lashed out at everyone and even lost my best friend after beating him up. My father got me a punching bag, which I demolished in a week. When my grandmother tried to tell me about angels, I turned away. When my birthday came that fall, I didn't set an extra place.

Frank's death triggered an uncontrollable rage in me against anything that failed to reach perfection. I became obsessed with achieving all I could as fast as possible. In high school, I took out my aggression in football and wrestling, and became the best athlete on the teams. I studied just as compulsively, graduating third in my class with a scholarship to the state university.

I got a summer sales job and was working seven days a week from morning to night. Then I met Marie. She came to the door to hear my passionate spiel about the gadgets I was selling, and as soon as I looked into her pretty round face and big brown eyes, I was in love. I proposed to her on the spot. She laughed, but two years later we married.

With marriage, school and a part-time job, my pent-up energy found a positive outlet. After college my anger continued to burn. I worked for an import-export business and literally lived in my office for days on end. When I came home, I was too tired to pay any attention to Marie and our three children. By the time I was 30, I was vice president.

One Easter weekend, Marie came into the den where I was working late. "Jack, I'm leaving you. I think I want a divorce."

She explained that our marriage was a disaster, with a husband who shut her out of his life entirely. "I've already taken the kids to Mother's and I'm going to join them. It's up to you whether we come back." Then she walked out of the house.

I was so shocked I couldn't speak. It was like my brother dying all over again, and once more I didn't know until it was too late. I started opening cabinets and smashing everything in sight against the wall. *How could she do this to me?* I raged as bottles and utensils went flying.

The final cabinet had a stack of dishes I had used as a child. The sight of them brought back memories of my brother that made me want to cry. I set them on the kitchen table and threw them one by one at the sink. But when I came to the last dish, I couldn't pick it up. It was stuck to the table. I used both hands, but still couldn't pry it up.

I stood there panting and sweating, my hands bleeding from a drinking glass I'd smashed. Suddenly, I heard a voice echo around me. "Jack, make room for me at the table."

It was kind and compassionate and sounded like a female voice, yet I felt a shiver of fear run through me. I sat down and cried until my head pounded and I couldn't cry anymore. When I finally got up to wash my face, I noticed the kitchen was in shambles. As I looked at that one remaining dinner plate, I heard the voice again, the most beautiful voice, like a soprano singing softly.

"Who are you?" I gasped.

"You know me, Jack," it replied. "Make room for me at your table."

Numb as I felt, I finally knew whose voice it was. This time I was able to pick up the plate without any problem, and I set it at the end where I usually sat. I placed a knife, fork and spoon around it, added a napkin and an aluminum drinking cup that had survived my rage, and pushed a chair in place.

As I sat looking at the place setting, I felt the most incredible peace I had ever known. Then I bowed my head and said the prayer I had learned with my brother: "Angel of God, my guardian dear...."

When I finished, I talked non-stop to the angel about my life for a good hour. I can't pretend I saw her across the table, but I felt my angel's presence just as I had heard her speak to me. And she was telling me now that my anger was gone, I could finally change my life.

The sky was beginning to lighten when I heard the sound of a key in the lock. It was Marie. She surveyed the kitchen in horror. Then she threw her arms around me. "I couldn't sleep," she cried. "It was as if I heard a voice saying over and over, 'Jack needs you, Marie.' So I came." Marie washed and bandaged my hands, then put me to bed without saying another word.

Marie spent hours cleaning up before I woke. As I started to apologize, she shook her head. "Just tell me," she said. "Why did you break everything in the kitchen, then go to the trouble of setting the table?"

When I finished my story, she looked thoughtful. "Somehow you *are* different, Jack," she commented. "The tension is gone."

"Marie, I hope this doesn't seem silly," I began, "but I want to keep that place setting on the table forever. If my angel hadn't come last night, I don't know what I might have done. I want to keep reminding myself of something I knew when I was a kid but forgot."

That strange night was two decades ago, but its effects have stayed with me. Marie and I took the first vacation since our honeymoon and began to rebuild our marriage. In 1992, we celebrated our 35th wedding anniversary. Our three children have families of their own, so we now have six grandchildren on earth and one waiting for us in heaven. I left my job to start my own business and found pleasure, instead of compulsion, in work again.

And each night, I still set out the old plate and dented aluminum cup, the silverware and napkin. They're a pledge to my guardian angel, and to God who sent her, that she will always be welcome at my table.

Faith furnishes prayer with wings, without which it cannot soar to heaven.

ST. JOHN CLIMACUS

THE CELLIST OF SARAJEVO

BY

PAUL SULLIVAN

As a pianist, I was invited to perform with cellist Eugene Friesen at the International Cello Festival in Manchester, England. Every two years a group of the world's greatest cellists and others devoted to that unassuming instrument—bow makers, collectors, historians—gather for a week of workshops, master classes, seminars, recitals and parties. Each evening the 600 or so participants assemble for a concert.

The opening-night performance at the Royal Northern College of Music consisted of works for unaccompanied cello. There on the stage in the magnificent concert hall was a solitary chair. No piano, no music stand, no conductor's podium. This was to be cello music in its purest, most intense form. The atmosphere was supercharged with anticipation and concentration.

The world-famous cellist Yo-Yo Ma was one of the performers that April night in 1994, and there was a moving story behind the musical composition he would play:

On May 27, 1992, in Sarajevo, one of the few bakeries that still had a supply of flour was making and distributing bread to the starving, war-shattered people. At 4 p.m. a long line stretched into the street. Suddenly, a mortar shell fell directly into the middle of the line, killing 22 people and splattering flesh, blood, bone and rubble.

Not far away lived a 35-year-old musician named Vedran Smailovic. Before the war he had been a cellist with the Sarajevo Opera, a distinguished career to which he patiently longed to return. But when he saw the carnage from the massacre outside his window, he was pushed past his capacity to absorb and endure any more. Anguished, he resolved to do the thing he did best: make music. Public music, daring music, music on a battlefield.

For each of the next 22 days, at 4 p.m., Smailovic put on his full, formal concert attire, took up his cello and walked out of his apartment into the midst of the battle raging around him. Placing a plastic chair beside the crater that the shell had made, he played in memory of the dead Albinoni's Adagio in G minor, one of the most mournful and haunting pieces in the classical repertoire. He played to the abandoned streets, smashed trucks and burning buildings, and to the terrified people who hid in the cellars while the bombs dropped and bullets flew. With masonry exploding around him, he made his unimaginably courageous stand for human dignity, for those lost to war, for civilization, for compassion and for peace. Though the shellings went on, he was never hurt.

After newspapers picked up the story of this extraordinary man, an English composer, David Wilde, was so moved that he, too, decided to make music. He wrote a composition for unaccompanied cello, "The Cellist of Sarajevo," into which he poured his own feelings of outrage, love and brotherhood with Vedran Smailovic.

25

It was "The Cellist of Sarajevo" that Yo-Yo Ma was to play that evening.

Ma came out on stage, bowed to the audience and sat down quietly on the chair. The music began, stealing out into the hushed hall and creating a shadowy, empty universe, ominous and haunting. Slowly it grew into an agonized, screaming, slashing furor, gripping us all before subsiding at last into a hollow death rattle and, finally, back to silence.

When he had finished, Ma remained bent over his cello, his bow resting on the strings. No one in the hall moved or made a sound for a long time. It was as though we had just witnessed that horrifying massacre ourselves.

Finally, Ma looked out across the audience and stretched out his hand, beckoning someone to come to the stage. An indescribable electric shock swept over us as we realized who it was: Vedran Smailovic, the cellist of Sarajevo!

Smailovic rose from his seat and walked down the aisle as Ma left the stage to meet him. They flung their arms around each other in an exuberant embrace. Everyone in the hall erupted in a chaotic, emotional frenzy—clapping, shouting and cheering.

And in the center of it all stood these two men, hugging and crying unashamedly. Yo-Yo Ma, a suave, elegant prince of classical music, flawless in appearance and performance; and Vedran Smailovic, dressed in a stained and tattered leather motorcycle suit. His wild long hair and huge mustache framed a face that looked old beyond his years, soaked with tears and creased with pain.

We were all stripped down to our starkest, deepest humanity at encountering this man who shook his cello in the face of bombs, death and ruin, defying them all. It was the sword of Joan of Arc—the mightiest weapon of them all.

Back in Maine a week later, I sat one evening playing the piano for the residents of a local nursing home. I couldn't help contrasting this concert with the splendors I had witnessed at the festival. Then I was struck by the profound similarities. With his music the cellist of Sarajevo had defied death and despair, and celebrated love and life. And here we were, a chorus of croaking voices accompanied by a shopworn piano, doing the same thing. There were no bombs and bullets, but there was real pain—dimming sight, crushing loneliness, all the scars we accumulate in our lives—and only cherished memories for comfort. Yet still we sang and clapped.

It was then I realized that music is a gift we all share equally. Whether we create it or simply listen, it's a gift that can soothe, inspire and unite us, often when we need it most—and expect it least.

Sometimes our fate resembles a fruit tree in winter. Who would think that those branches would turn green again and blossom, but we hope it, we know it.

WOLFGANG VON GOETHE

FLIGHT OF THE RED-TAIL

BY
PENNY PORTER

The hawk hung from the sky as though suspended from an invisible web, its powerful wings outstretched and motionless. It was like watching a magic show—until, suddenly, the spell was shattered by a shotgun blast from the car behind us.

Startled, I lost control of my pickup. It careened across the gravel shoulder until we stopped inches short of a barbed-wire fence. My heart was pounding as the car raced past us, the steel muzzle of a gun sticking out the window. I shall never forget the gleeful smile on the face of the boy who'd pulled that trigger.

"Geez, Mom. That scared me!" said Scott, 14, sitting beside me. Then my son's face clouded. "Look! He shot that hawk!"

While driving home along Arizona's Interstate 10 to our cattle ranch, we had been marveling at a magnificent pair of red-tailed hawks swooping low over the Sonoran Desert. Cavorting and diving at breathtaking speeds, the beautiful birds mirrored each other in flight. Then one hawk changed its course and soared skyward, where it hovered for an instant over the interstate. That's when the gun blast turned their play into an explosion of feathers.

Horrified, we watched the red-tail spiral earthward straight into the path of an 18-wheeler. Air brakes screeched, but it was too late. The truck struck the bird, hurling it onto the median.

Scott and I ran to the spot where it lay. Because of the hawk's small size, we decided it was probably a male. He was on his back, a shattered wing doubled beneath him, the powerful beak open, and round, yellow eyes wide with pain and fear. The talons on his left leg had been ripped off, and where the brilliant fan of tail feathers had gleamed, only one red feather remained.

"We gotta do something, Mom."

"Yes," I murmured. "We've got to take him home."

As Scott reached for him, the terrified hawk lashed out with his one remaining weapon—a hooked beak as sharp as an ice pick. Scott threw his leather jacket over the bird, wrapped him firmly and carried him to the pickup. From somewhere high in the sky, we heard the plaintive, high-pitched cry of the other hawk. "What will that one do now, Mom?"

"I don't know," I replied. "I've heard they mate for life."

At the ranch, we tackled our first problem: restraining the flailing hawk without getting hurt ourselves. Wearing welding gloves, we laid him on some straw inside an orange crate and slid the slats over his back.

Once the bird was immobilized, we removed splinters of bone from his shattered wing and then tried bending the wing where the main joint had been. It would fold only halfway. Through all this pain, the hawk never moved. The only sign of life was an occasional raising of the third lid over fear-glazed eyes.

With the blind faith of youth, Scott made the decision

Wondering what to do next, I called the Arizona-Sonora Desert Museum. "I know you mean well," the curator said sympathetically, "but euthanasia is the kindest thing."

"Destroy him?" I asked, gently stroking the auburn-feathered bird secured in the crate.

"He'll never fly again with a wing that badly injured," he continued. "Even if he could, he'd starve to death. Hawks need their claws as well as their beaks to tear up food."

As I hung up, I knew he was right.

"But the hawk hasn't even had a chance to fight," Scott argued.

Fight for what? I wondered. To huddle in a cage? Never to fly again?

With the blind faith of youth, Scott made the decision for us. "Maybe, by some miracle, he'll fly again," he said. "Isn't it worth the try?"

So began a weeks-long vigil during which the bird never moved, ate or drank. We forced water into his beak with a syringe, but the pathetic creature just lay there, scarcely breathing. Then came the morning when the red-tail's eyes were closed.

"Mom, he's ... dead!" Scott cried.

"Maybe some whiskey," I said. It was a technique we'd used before to coax an animal to breathe. We pried open the beak and poured a teaspoon of the liquid down the hawk's throat. Instantly his eyes flew open and his head fell into the water bowl in the cage.

"Look, Mom! He's drinking!" Scott said, with tears sparkling in his eyes.

By nightfall, the hawk had eaten several strips of steak, sprinkled with sand to ease digestion. The next day Scott removed the bird from the crate and wrapped his good claw around a fireplace log where he teetered and swayed until the talons locked in. As Scott let go of the bird, the good wing flexed slowly into flight position, but the other was rigid, protruding from his shoulder like a boomerang. We held our breath until the hawk stood erect.

The creature watched every move we made, but the look of fear was gone. He was going to live. Now, would he learn to trust us?

With Scott's permission, his three-year-old sister, Becky, named our visitor Hawkins. We put him in a chain-link dog-run ten feet high and open at the top. That way he'd be safe from bob-cats, coyotes, raccoons and lobos. In one corner we mounted a manzanita limb four inches from the ground. The crippled bird perched there day and night, staring at the sky, watching, listening, waiting.

In time, Hawkins's growing trust blossomed into affection. We delighted in spoiling him with treats like baloney and beef jerky soaked in sugar water. Soon, the hawk whose beak was powerful enough to crush the skull of a desert rat had mastered the touch of a butterfly. Becky fed him with her bare fingers.

Hawkins loved to play games. His favorite was tug of war. With an old sock gripped tight-ly in his beak and one of us pulling on the other end, he always won, refusing to let go even when Scott lifted him into the air. Becky's favorite was ring-around-the-rosy. She and I held hands and circled Hawkins's pen, while his eyes followed until his head turned 180 degrees. He was actually looking at us backward!

We grew to love Hawkins. We talked to him. We stroked his satiny feathers. We had saved and tamed a wild creature. *But now what?* Shouldn't we return him to the sky, to the world where he belonged?

Scott must have been wondering the same thing, even as he carried his pet around on his wrist like a proud falconer. One day he raised Hawkins's perch just over the bird's head. "If he has to struggle to get up on it, he might get stronger," Scott said.

Noticing the height difference, Hawkins assessed the change from every angle. He jumped—and missed, landing on the concrete, hissing pitifully. He tried again and again with the same result. Just as we thought he'd given up, he flung himself up at the limb, grabbing first with his beak, then his claw, and pulled. At last he stood upright.

Each week after that, Scott raised the perch a little more, until Hawkins sat proudly at four feet. How pleased he looked—puffing himself up and preening. But four feet was his limit; he could jump no higher.

Spring brought warm weather and birds: doves, quail, road runners and cactus wrens. We thought Hawkins would enjoy all the chirping and trilling. Instead, we sensed a sadness in our hawk.

One morning we found him perched with his good wing extended, the other quivering helplessly. All day he remained in this position, a piteous, rasping cry coming from his throat. Finally we saw what was troubling him: high in the sky over his pen, another red-tail hovered.

His mate? I asked myself. *How could it be?* We were at least 30 miles from where we'd found Hawkins, far beyond a hawk's normal range. Had his mate somehow followed him here? Or, through some secret of nature, did she simply know where he was?

"What will she do when she realizes he can't fly?" Scott asked.

"I imagine she'll get discouraged and leave," I said sadly. "We'll just have to wait and see."

Our hopes, like

towering falcons,

Aim at objects in an

airy height.

CHARLES MONTAGUE

Our wait was brief. The next morning Hawkins was gone.

Questions tormented us. How did he get out? The only possibility was that he'd simply pulled himself six feet up the fence, grasping the wire first with his beak, then his one good claw. Next he must have fallen ten feet to the ground.

How would he survive? He couldn't hunt. Clinging to his perch and a strip of meat with one claw had proven nearly impossible. Our crippled hawk would be easy prey. We were heartsick.

A week later, however, there was Hawkins perched on the log pile by our kitchen door. His eyes gleamed with a brightness I'd never seen before. And his beak was open. "He's hungry!" I shouted. The bird snatched a package of baloney from Scott's hand and ate greedily.

Finished, Hawkins hopped awkwardly to the ground. We watched as he lunged, floated and crashed in short hops across the pasture, one wing flapping mightily, the other a useless burden. Journeying in front, his mate swooped back and forth, scolding and whistling her encouragement until he reached the temporary safety of a mesquite grove.

Hawkins returned to be fed throughout the spring. Then one day, instead of taking his food, he shrank back and squawked. Suddenly he struck at us with his beak. The hawk that had trusted us for nearly a year was now afraid. I knew he was ready to return to the wild.

As the years passed, we occasionally saw a lone red-tail gliding across our pastures, and my heart would leap with hope. Had Hawkins somehow survived? And if he hadn't, was it worth the try to keep him alive as we did?

Nine years later, when Scott was 23, he met an old friend in Phoenix who had lived near our ranch. "You won't believe this," he said, "but I think I saw your hawk roosting in a scrub oak down by the wash. He was all beat up with a broken wing, just like Hawkins."

"You gotta go take a look, Mom," insisted Scott.

The next day I drove north until the dirt road became zigzagging cattle trails and finally no trails at all. When a barricade of thorny mesquite trees stopped me, it was time to walk. Finally an opening through the maze led me down to a sandy wash. This was an Eden for lizards, toads, tarantulas and snakes. It was also the perfect feeding ground for a hawk.

I searched for hours, but saw no trace of Hawkins. Finding him, I thought, was too much to hope for. It was getting cold when I sensed I was being watched. Suddenly I found myself looking straight into the eyes of a large female red-tail. Roosting in a mesquite less than 15 feet away, she was perfectly camouflaged by autumn foliage.

Could this magnificent creature have been Hawkins's mate? I wanted so much to believe she was, to tell Scott I had seen the bird that had cared for her mate, scavenged for his food and kept him safe. But how could I be sure?

Then I saw him.

On a branch beneath the dark shadow of the larger bird hunched a tattered little hawk. When I saw the crooked wing, the proud bald head and withered claw, my eyes welled with tears. This was a magic moment: a time to reflect on the power of hope. A time to bless the boy with faith.

Alone in this wild place, I learned the power of believing, for I had witnessed a small miracle.

"Hawkins," I whispered, longing to stroke the ragged feathers, but daring only to circle him. "Is it really you?" My answer came when the yellow eyes followed my footsteps until he was looking at me backward and the last rays of sunlight danced on his one red feather.

Then, finally, I knew—and, best of all, my son would know. It *had* been worth the try.

Hold fast to dreams,

for if dreams die,

life is a broken-winged bird

that cannot fly.

LANGSTON HUGHES

MESSAGE IN A STARRY SKY

BY

ANNETTE BASLAW-FINGER

We were at the close of a wonderful vacation at our rented summer house. Ten years old, brimming with happiness, I ran in from the beach and found my parents in each other's arms. Both had tears in their eyes.

"What's wrong?" I asked, my heart pounding. I had never seen my parents cry before.

"We are at war," my father explained. Though I had only a vague notion of what war meant, I knew our lives would never be the same.

I had grown up in Paris in a gracious apartment full of paintings, books, antiques—and love. Fourteen years earlier, my father had come, penniless, from Vilnius, Lithuania, to attend medical school in France. There he met my mother, a philosophy student, also from Vilnius. Papa left school to marry *Maman*, and went into the leather-goods business with my Uncle Jack, the husband of his sister Gitel. Their daughter, Frances, 2 1/2 years my junior, was like a sister to me.

My aunt and uncle lived close by, and we shared vacations and holidays. I especially liked Hanukkah, the December holiday in which Jews commemorate the miracle that took place over two millennia ago. One day's supply of oil had miraculously kept the Eternal Light burning for eight days in the Temple at Jerusalem after the Jews had recaptured it from the Syrian Greeks. My father taught me that Hanukkah symbolized the steadfastness of faith under oppression. "Do not betray our past," Papa said. "Live with integrity to be a source of inspiration to future generations."

We prized our antique silver menorah, the nine-socket candelabrum that symbolizes the ancient oil lamp. During Hanukkah the whole family would stand around as my father ceremoniously lit the center candle, or shamas, from which we would light one additional candle each night until, on the last day, all were ablaze.

The high point of the evening for Frances and me was spinning the dreidel, a four-sided top with Hebrew letters on each side signifying, "A great miracle happened there." Depending on which letter the top landed on, the players could win candies. Our parents were on one team and Frances and I on the other. Somehow we children always won, and my father would tease me. "Mottele," he'd say, using my nickname, "she always gets the *gimel*, I don't understand how!" Afterwards, as I snuggled in my bed, I would fall asleep feeling I was the luckiest girl in the world.

Now, on that September afternoon in 1939, those safe and happy years had ended. The following spring the Germans began bombing Paris. Our family and Uncle Jack's took refuge on a remote farm about 1 1/2 hours from Paris. Before leaving, my mother told me to choose one plaything. Tears streaming down my face, I surveyed my books and toys. Finally I selected Rebecca, a fine porcelain doll with a pink dress and Shirley Temple curls. I clutched my mother's hand and lugged Rebecca to drown my sobs as we left. Somehow I knew I'd never see my home again.

We stayed at the farm only a few months. The Germans occupied northern France, making it dangerous for Jews in that area. We fled

It's our only chance, I was convinced that God's arm was around us protecting us.

south. For weeks we traveled from village to village, avoiding night raids and street searches.

One day, when the police were about to close in, the only place to hide was a windowless cellar. Before we went down, my father called me over to him.

"Mottele," he said, "we may have to remain inside for a long while. We have to find ways to remember how special this world is." He pretended to take an imaginary object off a shelf. "Let's open a memory bottle," he continued. "We will put into it only the sights, smells and moments that are most precious to us."

Papa made me walk barefoot through the grass to remember how it felt. I smelled different kinds of flowers, then closed my eyes and recalled the fragrance. We concentrated on the color of the sky and the feel of the breeze. "Now we will put all this into the memory bottle and put the cork in," he said, gesturing. The serenity of his smile gave me hope and strength.

We stayed in that basement for days. Whenever I felt despondent, Papa would say, "Pull the cork and take out a memory." Sometimes I'd take out a patch of blue sky, sometimes the scent of a rose, and always I felt better. Even after we came out of hiding, I used the memory bottle to sustain me through dark moments.

In October 1940 we went to the city of Toulouse, where we hid for several months in a dark, roach-infested room. Aunt Gitel was pregnant but couldn't see a doctor. (My little cousin Eugene would be born while we were still in hiding.) Frances and I could not attend school. We children overheard our parents whispering about Jews being rounded up by the Vichy French authorities and being "deported."

As the persecution intensified, our situation became perilous. One option was to try to reach Spain, where, we were told, Jewish refugees were being accepted. But if we got caught at the border, we would surely be deported.

On the day before my 13th birthday, we held a family conference. Uncle Jack favored risking the escape. I had never seen Papa so torn. Finally he looked at me and asked, "Mottele, what do you say?"

For the first time I was invited to participate in a grown-up decision. "We have to go, Papa," I answered. "It's our only chance." I was convinced that God's arm was around us, protecting us.

"Well, then, it's decided. We'll go," Papa said. Two days after our trek began, the Germans occupied the rest of the country.

Furtively we moved across southern France, avoiding police blockades and German platoons. We slept in attics, basements and back rooms, always fearing someone might report us. At last we arrived at the foot of the snow-capped Pyrenees, where Papa and Uncle Jack gave half of all we had to two guides who promised to lead us over the mountains into Spain.

"Papa, I can't climb a mountain," I blurted, frightened at the daunting peak looming above. Papa put his arm around me. "Don't worry, Mottele," he said. "Just take one step. After that, you'll take another, then another. Before you know it, you will have made it."

Our chief guide, a thin, curt man with a nervous twitch in one eye, set the rules: "We climb at night and hide during the day. *Adelante y pronto*—forward and fast." Those three words, repeated in a harsh, disembodied whisper, drove us mercilessly.

Soon we were groping at steep rocks, slipping, grabbing at twigs as we climbed. At times I had to hold my doll, Rebecca, in my teeth to keep my hands free. A bitter wind slashed through my thin jacket, freezing me to the bone. Silently, I wept.

When we got to a high plateau at daybreak, the two guides told us to rest while they scouted ahead.

They never returned.

Now we were stranded on an unfamiliar mountaintop. "We have to make it on our own," Papa said. As we climbed the seemingly endless mountains, however, we failed to find a way down. We were getting colder and hungrier. By the second day we had only one crust of bread left, which Aunt Gitel fed to Eugene. Frances and I looked on, drooling.

On the third night, Papa suddenly lost his footing and slid down a slope. In the faint moonlight I saw him come to a stop in a ravine some 30 feet below. He tried to get up but couldn't. Finally he called, "Go on without me! I'll follow later."

Some miraculous flow of adrenalin propelled me down to him. "You must get up!" I pleaded. "We can't go on without you. Please—I'll help!"

Papa looked at me. Then, holding my arm, he slowly rose. Step by step, we made our way to the others. The deathly pallor on his face showed the pain he was suffering.

A new calm came over me. In helping my father, I had conquered my fear. I had grown up a little.

At dawn of the fifth day we finally saw the roofs of a village below. On all our minds hung the silent question, "What if it's still France?"

We fearfully headed for the hamlet. Then we noticed a sign: *panadería*—bakery, in Spanish! We shouted and hugged each other. We had made it!

Papa went to the local authorities. "Do you have entry papers?" the official asked. Of course, we did not. "Then I will make believe I did not see you, but you must leave immediately," the official said.

What now? If we were caught and sent back to France, it meant sure

The word which God has written on the brow of every man is Hope.

VICTOR HUGO

deportation. "We'll head for Portugal," the adults decided. "It's our only hope." For days we trudged across northern Spain, walking by night and hiding by day. We ate what we found in the fields.

One evening in December 1942, we stopped for shelter in a cow barn. It was cold, and we were desperately hungry. We had only a single stringy carrot that we had found in a muddy field.

As I sat next to Papa on a sheaf of straw, I began feeling sorry for myself. I was tired of being hungry and dirty. I'd had enough of sleeping on straw. I longed for a return to family life in a safe, stable place.

What's more, I knew it was about the time of Hanukkah. Memories began crowding in on me. On the verge of tears, I put my head on my father's shoulder. "We don't even have Hanukkah candles to light," I blurted between sobs.

"What do you mean?" Papa replied. "We have the most beautiful menorah in the world. God gave it to us." With that he opened the barn door just a crack. Peeking out, I saw a sky black as velvet sprinkled with glittering stars. "Pick out the shamas," Papa whispered. "Make sure it's the brightest."

It took a while to decide. Eventually I settled on the most luminous star I saw. Then Papa said, "Now pick out the other eight." Visualizing our menorah at home, I chose four stars on each side of the shamas. We made believe we lit the first star, then Father shut the door.

"Who has the dreidel?" Papa now asked the family. With a theatrical gesture he put his hand behind his back and quickly brought it forth, calling "Come on, let's play."

As we gathered, Father produced our one carrot and placed it in the middle. "All right. Let's see who wins it." I reached for the imaginary dreidel and made believe I was spinning it for my partner Frances and me. As I "let go," everyone seemed to hold his breath to see where it would fall.

"Mottele, you've won it all!" Papa finally called out, and ceremoniously handed me the carrot. Frances beamed with triumph, and the grownups feigned disappointment, just as they had in happier days.

A carrot that only a few minutes before had been a symbol of deprivation suddenly became a wonderful prize. I picked it up as if it were the most precious object, broke it into small pieces and divided it equally among the family. When I bit into my portion, it tasted of sugar like the sweets from my early childhood.

Later, when I burrowed into the straw to go to sleep, my heart was filled with happiness. From having nothing at all, I had passed to having more than I could measure—untold riches of hope and love. Steadfastness and faith through adversity, the meaning and reward of Hanukkah, had never been clearer.

"A great miracle happened there," I whispered as I fell asleep. "And God gave me a miracle today."

We finally reached the border, and for a few months we stayed in a refugee reception center in Portugal, while friends in America got us papers. I will never forget the whiteness of the bread in the sandwich that was handed me on the day we arrived in Philadelphia, August 23, 1943.

"One step at a time" we learned English and began a new existence. My sister Gaby was born nine months after we reached America. Over the years I married, had a family of my own, obtained a Ph.D., and became a foreign-languages professor. Today I'm the proud grandmother of four.

Rebecca, a bit worse for wear, went to one of my daughters when she was born. My three children all have memory bottles. I keep filling mine, as Papa taught me, with exquisitely precious moments. And each time I walk under a starry sky, I look up and search for our menorah, and feel God's arm around me.

True hope is swift, and flies with

swallow's wings:

Kings it makes gods, and meaner

creatures kings.

WILLIAM SHAKESPEARE

LIFE'S EXTRAS

BY

ARCHIBALD RUTLEDGE

One October night I walked down my seaside village street on a sad mission, to visit a friend lying very sick. But there was a full moon, and I felt the silver of it quiet my heart. The world lay lustrous: every scrawny bush and stone was transfigured. A breeze carried marshy odors over the brimming salt tide.

I found my friend, too, aware of the beauty of the night. From his window he could see the glamour, the light flooding the tide and running white lances through the trees. As I sat beside him, a mockingbird began to sing in the moonlight.

Long afterward my friend said to me, "I thought that night would be my last. But from the time the bird song came through the window, I knew I would get well." On the table by his bed had been all the necessities for a sick man; he had small comfort from them. Yet the moonlight, and the hale fragrances, and the wild song of the bird—these brought solace. He said, "I don't talk much about such things, but I felt all that beauty and peace was really the love of God."

I thought about this a great deal. And it seemed to me clear that creation provides necessities—sunlight, air, water, food—that we need to survive. But moonlight and starlight are distinctly extras. Music, perfumes, colors are extras. Who put them here, and for what purpose? The wind is perhaps a necessity; the song it blows through the pines is a quite different thing.

My knowledge of theology is primitive. Still, I am absolutely unshaken in my belief that God ministers to our spirits by the beauty that adorns creation. Indeed, thinking this way about life's extras has done more to help my faith than all the sermons I ever heard.

I once had a curious experience with a star. I was on the path to my farm at dusk when I was overtaken by a violent storm. The rain came down into howling darkness; the thunder and lightning were appalling. A bolt struck a pine 20 feet from me. The tree crashed down. Alone I was, defenseless, in the profound fury of the wind.

I squinted through the heavy rain toward what I believed was the west. To my amazement, I saw a rift in the inky blackness hardly bigger than my hand, and in the very heart of it gleamed the evening star. In faithful stillness and peace it shone, saying to my heart: "This storm is only temporary. The sky is here, and the stars."

Amid the chaos about me, here came a celestial message. Shining through the storm, its light reminded me of something past our world. Taking heart, I waded out to the road, headed homeward through the breaking storm, and reached the house in full, calm starlight.

Stars always fill me with a sense of God; I cannot help being grateful. The human mind may be inclined to reject this kind of proof of God's love. But the human heart can hardly do so. In things spiritual the heart is the better guide.

I know a certain old hunter, an obscure man as far as the world is concerned, but a loyal friend. Occasionally he will tell me something intimate about himself; and when he does, it is usually remarkable, as I believe the following story is.

"It happened one June," my friend told me. "Bill Moore and I, see, had trouble between us for years. The last time we met, if friends hadn't separated us, we'd have finished the thing right there.

"After that night, I figured one of us would get the other. I knew he  carried a gun, and I began to do the same. Well, that day in June one of my friends told me Bill said he was planning to kill me. I made up my mind to meet him a little more than halfway, and late that afternoon I walked up toward Bill's house, intending to get it over with.

"A mile from his house, I saw somebody coming down the road. I stepped aside into one of the bay branches and stood still, with the bushes all around me, my hand on the gun and the devil in my heart. I put up my left hand to pull aside a limb, when on it I saw a white flower, a sweet bay flower.

"You'll think I was a fool, but I leaned over and smelled it. My mother used to love that flower; and when I was a boy she made me bring a bush from the swamp and plant it in the yard. She was buried with one of the flowers in her hand. I got to thinking about the kind of man she hoped I might be.

"Then, first thing I knew, Bill was opposite me in the road. But something had happened—I didn't want to harm him now. I stepped out of the bushes, calling to him. Something in the way I came up made him know it was all right. And it was all right, because we made it right, then and there. Now what do you think of that—and all because of a flower? But it's the truth, just as I'm telling you."

He "redeemeth thy life from destruction," says the Psalmist, but we do not often think of the deft ways in which God works. Beauty is made to touch the heart, the spirit is renewed, and life is reclaimed.

One day I walked into the woods to try to escape my grief over the loss of one dearly loved. A little way in, I heard a warbler. He was in the crest of a bald cypress, high over a woodland lake. All around me was music: a stream splashing over the roots of pines, the wind in tall grasses. Everywhere I looked I saw wild, sequestered grace.

What did the music and the beauty, those extras, bring me? Slowly moving from keen sorrow I came to a quiet reconciliation—to the conviction that, living or dying, God will take care of us.

In those woods I saw both life and death—in the green leaves and the brown, in the standing trees and the fallen. If you are honest when you ask the question, What dies? you must answer, Everything the eye sees. In the woods, surrounded by those things God provided, I understood that if we are to hold on to anything—and in sorrow we must have something we can cling to—it must be to the unseen.

For the strength that is permanent, we have to lean on faith; for immortal hope, we have to trust, not the things that we behold but those invisible things that our hearts know.

Whatever my religion may be worth, I feel deeply that life's extras have given it to me; and time shall not take it from me. Nor have I come to this by sunny paths alone. I know well the valley of the shadow of death; I know the veil which sight cannot pierce. But I know, also, from the great beauty we so freely enjoy, that behind the veil is a God of mercy and of tenderest love.

"YOU'LL BE A MAN, MY SON!"

BY

SUZANNE CHAZIN

$\mathcal{T}$he rumpled, brown-paper package was addressed simply to "Monsieur Kipling." Rudyard Kipling, celebrated British author and Nobel Prize-winner, opened it, his curiosity piqued by the painstaking scrawl. Inside was a red box containing a French translation of his novel *Kim*—pierced by a bullet hole that stopped at the last 20 pages. Through the hole, tied with string, dangled the Maltese Cross of the Croix de Guerre, France's medal for bravery in war.

The book had been sent by a young French soldier, Maurice Hamonneau. He explained in a letter that had *Kim* not been in his pocket when he went into battle, he would have been killed. Hamonneau asked Kipling to accept the book and medal as a token of gratitude.

Kipling felt more moved than he had been by any other honor he'd received. Through him, God had spared the life of this soldier. If only he had spared the life of another—one who meant more to Kipling than all the honors in the world.

Twenty-one years before, in the summer of 1897, Kipling's American wife, Carrie, bore their third child. The Kiplings already had two daughters, Josephine and Elsie, whom Rudyard adored. He hoped for a boy this time. He would always remember the moment that high-pitched squeal rang out. "Mr. Kipling," the doctor called, "you have a son!"

Soon Kipling was gazing at an almost-nine-pound, swaddled bundle. He cradled the warm, yawning infant in his arms, and a yearning rose within him more profound than any he had ever known.

John Kipling, as they named the boy, turned out to be a bright, cheerful and uncomplaining child. Kipling felt blessed. But in the winter of 1899, tragedy struck.

On a trip to the United States, Rudyard and his older daughter, six-year-old Josephine, became ill with pneumonia. Before antibiotics, there was little doctors could do. On March 4, Kipling, desperately weak, finally pulled himself out of his delirium. Two days later, Josephine died.

Kipling could no longer bring himself to look at pictures of Josephine or hear her name mentioned. But he had to put aside his grief for the sake of three-year-old Elsie and 19-month-old John.

He took the children for picnics on the hilly Sussex Downs. He built a sandbox for them. When it came to playing with them, no game was too outlandish.

Kipling's fondest memories of those early years were the winters between 1900 and 1907, which the family spent near Cape Town, South Africa. On hot afternoons, Kipling would lie in a hammock in the shade of a huge oak tree, his children close by. "Daddo," John may have asked one such time, "why do leopards have spots?"

No doubt a sparkle came to Kipling's eyes. The leopard, he began, mimicking the voice of an ancient sage, had long ago been sandy-brown in color, as were the zebra and giraffe he hunted on the open savannas. But then, to foil the leopard, the zebra and giraffe hid in the forests.

"After a long time," Kipling continued, "what with standing half in the shade and half out of it, the giraffe grew blotchy, and the zebra grew stripy." The leopard, in order to hunt his new prey in the forest, needed to change too, explained Kipling, so he chose spots. "Now and then you will hear grownups ask, 'Can a leopard change his spots?'" Kipling winked at his children and shook his head no. "He is quite contented as he is."

Kipling collected his fantastical tales about wildlife into a book called *Just So Stories.* In 1902, the book was published to critical acclaim. He was fast becoming a favorite author of children around the world. Few would have guessed that the man who so loved the magic and mystery of childhood had had such an unhappy one himself.

Born in Bombay, India, in 1865, Rudyard Kipling first glimpsed the world through the bustling street life of India. But before he turned six, he and his younger sister Trix were shipped off to England to attend school. The woman paid to board them beat and taunted the small, frail Rudyard, and censored the children's letters home. Often she would lock him in a cold, damp cellar for hours.

Despite all the abuse, young Kipling willed himself to remain cheerful. Years later, he wrote that the experience "drained me of any capacity for real, personal hate for the rest of my days." It also made him all the more determined to give his own children the happiness, love and security he had lacked.

Kipling returned to India to become a newspaper reporter, and wrote fiction in his spare time. His plots dealt with the courage, sacri-

> *Hope is the*
> *parent of faith*
>
> C.A. BARTOL

fice and discipline he saw in British servicemen stationed there, as well as with the mystery and danger of India. He collected his popular stories into short books, hoping to find a market in London.

Editors there derided his work. One wrote: "I would hazard a guess that the writer is very young, and that he will die mad before he has reached the age of 30." Kipling ignored the criticism and continued to write. In time, as his books gained popularity with readers, he became sought after by famous writers, academics and politicians. Kipling, however, was as indifferent to the praise as he had been to the earlier criticism.

By the early 1900s, Kipling was predicting war with Germany and calling for compulsory military service. For this he was frequently mocked by critics as an "imperialist" and a "jingoist." Even though he was increasingly scorned by the thinkers of the day, Kipling stood firm in his views and drew strength from his home and family.

His son John was growing tall and handsome. Though not a skilled athlete, John loved competing in sports at his boarding school. How Kipling loved to watch his son, radiant with enthusiasm, dashing across the rugby field. How proud Kipling was—not because John was a great athlete but because he showed the quiet spunk and good humor that the father admired. John congratulated teammates and opponents on their efforts. He never bragged about a win or whined about a loss. If he broke a school rule, he took his punishment without complaint. He accepted responsibility for his actions. The boy, Kipling realized, was becoming a man.

To Kipling, that meant handling adversity with fortitude. He wanted to encourage this conduct in his son. If John could follow in the footsteps of great men Kipling had known, if he could live by that set of values, if….

On a winter's day in 1910, Kipling began to pen those thoughts for his 12-year-old son. He called the poem "If—," and included it in a book of children's tales published later that year.

The critics did not consider it one of his greatest works. Yet within a few short years, the four-stanza poem became a classic the world over, translated into 27 languages. Schoolchildren memorized it. Young men marching off to battle recited it. Its simple, inspirational code of conduct defined for millions of people a set of values to live by.

By 1915, the war Kipling had predicted was raging in Europe. His son John was now a tall, lean, quick-witted 17-year-old with nut-brown hair, sparkling hazel eyes and the wispy beginnings of a mustache. Since he had poor eyesight like his father, he was rejected as an officer by both the army and the navy. Eventually Kipling managed to get him a commission as a second lieutenant with the Irish Guards, which he eagerly accepted.

Shipped to Ireland, John proved an able officer. Meanwhile, Kipling campaigned on the home front for volunteers and visited France to write about the war.

In May, Britain was rocked by news of heavy casualties. As wave after wave of recruits went overseas, John's departure loomed nearer. Kipling knew he had a choice. Because John was only 17, he required parental consent to go to the front. But Kipling could not now shirk everything he'd taught his son to believe—no matter what the consequences. He gave his consent.

At noon on August 15, John waved good-by to his mother and sister with a tip of his officer's cap. Carrie Kipling wrote that he looked "very smart and straight and brave, as he turned to say, 'Send my love to Daddo,' " who was already in France.

Just over six weeks later, on October 2, a messenger arrived at the Kipling estate, bearing a telegram from the War Office. John was missing in action, last seen during a battle in Loos, France.

Kipling made desperate efforts to determine John's fate, but no one could supply any information. Unable to sit idly by, he trudged from one muddy outpost hospital to another, searching for wounded men from John's battalion. Quiet and self-effacing, he instantly established rapport with the soldiers he visited. Yet nothing could staunch the hollow wound that grew within him as months went by, and still no news came of his son.

Toward the end of 1917, an eyewitness was finally located who had seen John die two years earlier in the Battle of Loos. Even with this sad news, the family could not find relief, for John's body was never recovered.

During the remaining 18 years of his life, Kipling devoted himself to his duties as a member of the Imperial War Graves Commission, reburying—and honoring—the dead. He proposed the general inscription on the Stone of Sacrifice at each cemetery—"Their name liveth for evermore"—and the phrase "Known But Unto God" on the headstones of soldiers whose bodies, like that of his son, were never identified.

He visited countless sites and appeared at many functions on behalf of the commission. All the while, he was nearly overwhelmed by a feeling of hopelessness. He had sacrificed his greatest gift. For what purpose? On sleepless nights, when the timbered ceilings of his stone house creaked, Kipling sat in the darkness, trying to answer that question. For the first time in his life, the man who'd made his living by words could find none to ease his own pain.

On a journey to France, Kipling visited Maurice Hamonneau, the French soldier who had sent him his Croix de Guerre at the end of the war. Over the years, the two men had corresponded, and a friendship had bloomed. Then one day in 1929, Hamonneau wrote that his wife had given birth to a son. Would Kipling be the godfather?

He would be delighted, Kipling wrote back. It was only fitting, he added, that Hamonneau's copy of *Kim* and his medal be given to the boy.

Kipling stared out his study window, recalling that joyful moment when he first cradled his own son in his arms. Hamonneau now knew that magical feeling. God, through Kipling, had spared Hamonneau's life, and something miraculous had come from it all.

For the first time in years, Kipling felt a surge of hope. Here is what John had sacrificed his life for—the unborn. Of all the memorials Kipling could construct, none would do more justice to his courageous son's memory than this tiny infant, so full of life and promise.

"My son's name was John," he wrote to Hamonneau. "So yours must be Jean." And so it was that Kipling's godson bore the French version of his own son's name—and another father could know the hope and delight Kipling had felt, watching a son become a man.

If—

If you can keep your head when all about you
Are losing theirs and blaming it on you;
If you can trust yourself when all men doubt you,
But make allowance for their doubting too;
If you can wait and not be tired by waiting,
Or being lied about, don't deal in lies,
Or being hated don't give way to hating,
And yet don't look too good, nor talk too wise:

If you can dream—and not make dreams your master;
If you can think—and not make thoughts your aim,
If you can meet with Triumph and Disaster
And treat those two impostors just the same;
If you can bear to hear the truth you've spoken
Twisted by knaves to make a trap for fools,
Or watch the things you gave your life to, broken,
And stoop and build 'em up with worn-out tools:

If you can make one heap of all your winnings
And risk it on one turn of pitch-and-toss,
And lose, and start again at your beginnings
And never breathe a word about your loss;
If you can force your heart and nerve and sinew
To serve your turn long after they are gone,
And so hold on when there is nothing in you
Except the Will which says to them: 'Hold on!'

If you can talk with crowds and keep your virtue,
Or walk with Kings—nor lose the common touch,
If neither foes nor loving friends can hurt you,
If all men count with you, but none too much;
If you can fill the unforgiving minute
With sixty seconds' worth of distance run,
Yours is the Earth and everything that's in it,
And—which is more—you'll be a Man, my son!

I think it is difficult to say whether there is such a thing as hope or not. Hope is like a road in the country; there was never a road, but when many people walk on it, the road comes into existence.

LUSIN

THE DAY WE PLANTED HOPE

BY

CONRAD KIECHEL

We had just moved to France, and my wife Nancy and I were unpacking on a quiet August afternoon, busy making the rental apartment into a home for our uprooted family. At our feet our three-year-old, Claire, sat leafing through books. Far from friends and relatives, she was clearly tired of living with packing boxes.

"Please read me this," she said, thrusting a thin blue book in my direction. *It's Fun to Speak French* was stenciled on the spine of the faded cover. My grandfather, who had grown up speaking French, had given me the book when I was a child, and my parents had unearthed it from somewhere and sent it along with us.

Claire pointed to a page with line drawings below the bars of an old French children's song: "Do you know how to plant cabbages?" In blue ink, someone had crossed out cabbages and written "Watermelons!"

"Daddy! Did *you* do that?" Claire asked, looking up with an expression of shock. We had only recently convinced her not to write in books, and suddenly here was proof that her parents weren't practicing what they preached. I told her my grandfather had written in the book.

"Daddy!" Now she was really confused. "Why did your grandfather *do* that?" As I sat down to tell the story, my thoughts traveled a well-worn road back to Nebraska.

"Are we almost there?" my sister Vicky demanded from the back seat of our family's '54 Ford station wagon. It was the last, and toughest, day of our annual drive west to our grandparents' house perched above a creek bed in Tecumseh, Neb. For a few weeks each summer, Vicky and I had all the adventure we needed—working the old pump to see what kind of bugs came up in the water, choreographing fireworks displays in the back lot, escaping the midday sun under a canvas tarp thrown over two clotheslines.

When we pulled into their driveway, my grandmother burst from the back door to greet us. Behind her, Grandad hobbled over the lawn, then gathered us in his strong arms.

As a young man, Grandad had been a comer: a farmer, teacher, stockman and, at age 26, a Nebraska state senator. The trajectory of his life was straight up—until a massive stroke felled him at age 44 and crippled him for life. Sometime between his stroke and my boyhood, he had made peace with his life. His scrape with death had convinced him not how awful life is, but how precious. His zest for living made him a playmate Vicky and I fought over.

Each morning we pressed into Grandad's car for the drive to the post office, entertained along the way by the incessant patter of his nonsense rhymes: "Hello, Mrs. Brown. Why are *you* going to town?"

Best of all were trips to "the eighty," the only bit of farmland Grandad had managed to keep; the rest had been sold, or repossessed, to pay the bills in his years of recovery. Vicky and I would climb into

I watched my grand-father's joy take fresh root in her life

the barn's hayloft and, from an old cow stall below, Grandad made moo-ing noises that sent us into convulsions of laughter.

"I'm going to be a farmer too," I announced proudly one afternoon as Grandad sat playing solitaire at his desk.

Laying card upon card, he asked, "What are you going to grow?"

Suddenly I thought of a favorite pastime—spitting watermelon seeds as far as possible. "How about watermelons?" I asked.

"Hmm, there's a crop I haven't tried!" Brown eyes sparkling, he put his cards aside. "Better get your seeds in the ground quick though."

It was mid-August, and the days were growing shorter. Soon we would pack up for the drive back to Virginia—and school. I shuddered, feeling the first chill of autumn separation.

"Let's do it now!" I said, leaping out of my seat. "What do we do?"

First, Grandad said, we needed seeds. Remembering the slice of watermelon I'd seen in Aunt Mary's refrigerator, I raced out the door and across the yard to her house. In a flash I was back, five black seeds in my hand.

Grandad suggested a sunny spot in back of the house to plant the seeds. But I wanted a place where I could easily watch my plants' progress skyward.

We walked outside into the shade of a huge oak.

"Right here, Grandad," I said. I could sit with my back against the tree, reading comic books as the watermelons grew. It was perfect.

"Go to the garage and get the hoe," was Grandad's only reaction. Then he showed me how to prepare the ground and plant the seeds in a semicircle. "Don't crowd them," he said quietly. "Give them plenty of room to grow."

"Now what, Grandad?"

"Now comes the hard part," he said. "You wait." And for a whole afternoon, I did. Nearly every hour I checked on my watermelons, each time watering the seeds again. Incredibly, they had still not sprouted by suppertime, although my plot was a muddy mess. At the dinner table I asked Grandad how long it would take.

"Maybe next month," he said, laughing. "Maybe sooner."

The next morning I lay lazily in bed, reading a comic book. Suddenly, I remembered: *the seeds!* Dressing quickly, I ran outside.

What's that? I wondered, peering under the oak. Then I realized—*it's a watermelon!* A huge, perfectly shaped fruit lay nesting in the cool mud. I felt triumphant. *Wow! I'm a farmer!* It was the biggest melon I'd seen, and I'd grown it.

Just as I realized I hadn't, Grandad came out of the house. "You picked a great spot, Conrad," he chuckled.

"Oh Grandad!" I said. Then we quickly conspired to play the joke on others. After breakfast we loaded the melon into Grandad's trunk and took it to town, where he showed his cronies the "midnight miracle" his grandson had grown—and they let me believe they believed it.

Later that month Vicky and I got into the back seat of the station wagon for the glum ride back east. Grandad passed a book through the window. "For school," he said seriously. Hours later, I opened it to where he'd written "watermelons"—and laughed at another of Grandad's jokes.

Holding the book Grandad had given me that day long ago, Claire listened quietly to the story. Then she asked, "Daddy, can I plant seeds too?"

Nancy looked at me; together we surveyed the mountain of boxes waiting to be unpacked. About to say, "We'll do it tomorrow," I realized I had never heard Grandad say that. We took off for the market. At a small shop with a metal rack filled with seed packs, Claire picked one that promised bright red flowers, and I added a sack of potting soil.

On the walk home, while Claire munched a buttery croissant, I thought about those seeds I'd planted. For the first time I realized that Grandad could have met my childish enthusiasm with a litany of disappointing facts: that watermelons don't grow well in Nebraska; that it was too late to plant them anyway; that it was pointless to try growing them in the deep shade. But instead of boring me with the how of growing things, which I would soon forget, he made sure I first experienced the "wow."

Claire charged up the three flights of stairs to our apartment, and in a few minutes she was standing on a chair at the kitchen sink, filling a white porcelain pot with soil. As I sprinkled seeds into her open palm, I felt for the first time the pains Grandad had taken. He had stolen back into town that August afternoon and bought the biggest melon in the market. That night, after I was asleep, he had awkwardly unloaded it and, with a painful bend, placed it exactly above my seeds.

"Done, Daddy," Claire broke into my reverie. I opened the window over the sink and she put her pot on the sill, moving it from side to side until she found the perfect spot. "Now grow!" she commanded.

A few days later, shouts of "They're growing!" woke us, and Claire led us to the kitchen to see a pot of small green shoots. "Mommy," she said proudly, "I'm a farmer!"

I had always thought the midnight miracle was just another of Grandad's pranks. Now I realized it was one of his many gifts to me. In his refusal to let his crippling hinder him, he had planted something that neither time nor distance could uproot: a full-throttle grasping at the happiness life offers—and a disdain for whatever bumps get in the way.

As Claire beamed with satisfaction, I watched my grandfather's joy take fresh root in her life. And that was the biggest miracle of all.

Hopes, what are they?—Beads of morning

    Strung on slender blades of grass;

Or a spider's web adorning

    In a straight and treacherous pass.

WILLIAM WORDSWORTH

MIRACLE ON CHRISTMAS DAY

BY

DEBORAH MORRIS

Cold rain mixed with snow fell against the kitchen window of the house trailer in Elkins, W.Va. Melinda Eichelberger, seven months pregnant, pulled a tray of Christmas cookies from the oven. The frigid weather outside made the trailer a cozy haven on this night of December 23, 1990.

"Who wants a cookie?" Melinda called to Steve, 21, and their three-year-old daughter, Brittany, in the next room. Brittany quickly popped around the corner, wearing only a nightshirt and underwear. "I want one!" she said with a dimpled grin.

Melinda, 20, was taking time off from her restaurant job to catch up on Christmas baking. For once, she wouldn't have to rise at dawn to work the early shift. Steve, laid off from his discount-store job the week before, would also be home.

Around midnight, Melinda wearily turned off the oven. Steve was already in bed; Brittany was curled up on the floor, sound asleep. Their small Christmas tree twinkled brightly nearby.

66

Melinda smiled down at her daughter. *She looks so comfortable,* she thought. *I'll let her sleep here.* Covering Brittany with a blanket, she kissed her cheek and went to bed.

The night-stand clock read 9:33 a.m. when Melinda awoke with a start. *Oh, I don't have to work today,* she realized with relief. Then she noticed the house was unusually silent.

"Brittany?" she called sleepily as she shuffled down the hallway. The moment she stepped into the living room an icy draft hit her. She looked around in groggy confusion and saw the front door wide open. She pushed on the metal screen door. It was frozen in place. *Good,* Melinda thought with relief. *She couldn't have gone outside.*

"Brittany?" she called again. Melinda thought her daughter might be playing a joke. Two nights before, Brittany and Steve had hidden in the hall closet and jumped out to surprise her. But the closet was empty and so was Brittany's bedroom.

Melinda ran to wake Steve. "I can't find Brittany!" she cried. Together, they searched the trailer. Then Melinda's eyes turned to the door — and the wintry landscape outside.

"Oh dear God," she said. Throwing on jackets, the couple rushed out the door. The cold wind took their breath away. "Brittany!" they shouted, racing up and down the row of trailers. *Why didn't I wake up earlier?* Melinda thought. *Why didn't I hear her open the door? Please, God, don't let anything have happened to my baby.*

Then she spotted something between two trailers. "Steve!" she shrieked. Brittany, still clad only in her underwear and nightshirt, was lying in the snow. Her eyes were frozen open, wide and staring, her mouth agape. With her face framed by soft blond curls, she looked like a porcelain doll.

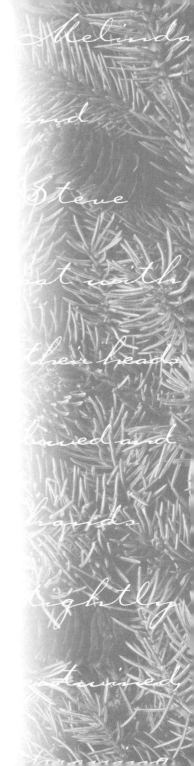

Steve scooped up his daughter and raced for their trailer, shouting for help. Brittany's tiny body was stiff, unyielding. He laid her on the couch and started piling blankets on her as a neighbor rushed in.

The man looked in horror at the waxy figure and glazed eyes, then checked for a pulse. Shaking his head, he placed both hands on her chest and began CPR. Steve, worried that Melinda would go into premature labor, sent her from the room with another neighbor.

The phone rang in the Randolph County Emergency Squad room. Minutes later an emergency crew pulled up in front of the trailer. Brenda Dailey, a paramedic and registered nurse, ran up the steps, her heart racing.

She shoved her way through the small crowd to the child's side. When her fingers touched Brittany's neck to check for a pulse, she gasped — the flesh was cold and hard. *She's frozen solid!* she thought in disbelief. Dailey moved the child to the floor and continued CPR.

A moment later paramedic Lora Eye and crew chief Delma Caudell rushed in with equipment. Caudell hooked up the child to a heart monitor. "She's got a flat line," she said grimly. As Steve turned away tearfully, Eye began chest compressions again. *Please, God,* she prayed silently. *It's Christmas Eve!*

The paramedics placed chemical hot packs on Brittany and then inserted a tube down her throat to force oxygen into her lungs. After they wrapped her with blankets and loaded her onto the stretcher, Steve followed them to the ambulance. Assured that a neighbor would drive Melinda to the hospital, he climbed in, and sirens began to wail.

Dr. John Veach was on duty in the emergency room at Davis

Memorial Hospital when Brittany arrived at 10:45 a.m. Her core temperature was 74 degrees Fahrenheit; her ice-glazed pupils were dilated and fixed. She had been in a deathlike state for at least 40 minutes.

The well-known rule in cases of severe cold, however, is that the victims aren't dead until they're warm and dead. "Get some heat lamps and a hypothermia blanket," Veach told the nurses.

After ordering a warm-water flush of the stomach, heated I.V. fluids, and warmed, humidified oxygen, Veach asked Eye and Dailey to continue CPR. Until Brittany's blood thawed enough to circulate freely, the cardiac drugs they had administered would have little effect.

Rushing into the room where Steve waited, Melinda clutched Brittany's favorite rag doll. "I thought she might want this," she said helplessly. Steve nodded, gently squeezing her hand.

Huddled on the couch, Melinda felt a fresh wave of pain as she thought of the gaily wrapped presents — a toy kitchen set, a cartoon video, some new crayons — hidden away for Christmas morning. Would Brittany ever get to open them? Would she be there when her baby brother or sister was born? Melinda and Steve sat with their heads bowed and hands tightly entwined, praying for a miracle.

For more than two hours, in the stifling heat of the eight lamps trained on Brittany, nurses and paramedics performed CPR. As the child's temperature approached 80 degrees with still no sign of life, the atmosphere in the emergency room grew increasingly tense. The unspoken thought hung in the air: *It's time to give up.*

No one wanted to stop, however. Maybe it was because of the devastated young parents outside, or simply because it was Christmas Eve. They continued to fight — forcing the child's stilled heart to beat, her empty lungs to fill.

At about 1 p.m. Lora Eye noticed blood and mucus trickling from Brittany's nose and mouth. "Look!" she said excitedly. "It's like she's starting to thaw!" Soon the heart monitor showed a subtle change — an uneven curve instead of a flat line.

Over the next hour the screen showed increasing heart activity. At 2:15 p.m., Dr. Veach touched Brittany's neck. "I've got a pulse!" he exclaimed. Against all odds, the little girl's heart was beating on its own.

Lora Eye smiled at Brenda Dailey and the other nurses. But even in that triumphant moment she felt a pang of doubt. The child had gone without oxygen for a long time — had they brought her back to a hopeless, vegetative existence? She quickly shook off the thought. *We did what we were trained to do*, she decided. *The rest is in God's hands.*

Melinda and Steve looked up fearfully when Veach walked in. "We've got your daughter's heart going again," he said. "We're transferring her to Children's Hospital in Pittsburgh." The couple followed the doctor down the hall to see their daughter.

Melinda gasped. Brittany was wrapped in a warm cocoon of blankets and aluminum foil to conserve body heat during the trip; only her blue lips and nose were visible. Her body jerked rhythmically as a nurse squeezed oxygen into her lungs. Both eyes were taped closed. All the nurses were crying.

Stepping forward, Melinda shakily laid Brittany's doll next to her. "Mommy's here," she whispered. "You're going to be okay." Minutes later the child was whisked to an ambulance. She'd be driven to a nearby airport, then flown to Pittsburgh.

As Eye and Dailey lifted Brittany into the vehicle, she groaned and tossed her head side to side. They talked soothingly, more from habit than from conviction that she understood. "Brittany's a good girl," Eye said. "Santa Claus is coming to see her." The child grew still, seeming to listen. Eye looked at Dailey quizzically before trying again: "Is Santa Claus coming to see Brittany?" This time the toddler seemed to nod slightly.

"I don't believe it!" Dailey exclaimed. "We must be imagining things." They experimented by singing "Jingle Bells" and "Frosty the Snowman." Each time they stopped, the little girl thrashed about restlessly. All the way to the airport the paramedics sang Christmas carols to the cold, distant child.

At Children's Hospital in Pittsburgh, Dr. Shekhar Venkataraman, a pediatric intensive-care physician, received word that a toddler with severe cold injuries was being airlifted in. The doctor shook his head; such tragedies were always wrenching. There was one positive factor, however: severe cold injuries sometimes have surprising outcomes.

For God alone my soul waits in silence, for my hope is from Him.

PSALM 62

When Brittany arrived at 4:30 p.m., Venkataraman tried to assess the child's neurological condition. She didn't respond even to painful stimuli, and her pupils didn't react to light.

Melinda and Steve, who had been driven to Pittsburgh by relatives, rushed into the hospital two hours later. "Your daughter's on a respirator, and her heart rate and blood pressure are becoming stabilized," Venkataraman told them, "but she's still very cold — only 84 degrees. We won't be able to run an EEG to evaluate her brain activity until she's a lot warmer."

As dusk fell on Christmas Eve, the couple began a silent vigil at their daughter's bedside. Melinda's eyes blurred with tears as she looked at Brittany's face, so beautiful and so still. *Please, God,* she prayed, *let her be okay.*

Then, early Christmas morning, the toddler's eyes suddenly fluttered open. "Brittany?" Melinda said breathlessly. "Can you hear me?" The eyes closed again, but Melinda was certain she had understood. "She's going to be okay," she told Steve excitedly. "I just know it!"

Brittany seemed to grow more alert as the day wore on. Several times it looked as though she was trying to focus on Melinda's face.

"She's coming around pretty quickly," Venkataraman told Melinda and Steve, "but until we take her off the respirator and see if she recognizes you, we won't be able to assess how much brain damage has occurred."

The next afternoon, Venkataraman and several nurses gathered around Brittany's bed in the ICU. As Melinda waited nearby, they carefully slid the respirator tube from Brittany's throat. She coughed and gagged for a moment, then began to cry and call out, "Mommy, Mommy!"

Melinda rushed to Brittany's bedside. As she tearfully kissed her daughter, the doctor and nurses watched with wide grins. The Christmas they had missed in a torment of doubt and despair had finally come, bearing the priceless gift of a child's life renewed.

Brittany's discolored skin soon regained its normal color. Physical therapy restored full use of her hands and feet, and helped offset an equilibrium problem that occasionally left her off-balance. By the time her sister, Kristin, was born in March, Brittany was walking and playing again, a happy three-year-old.

Today Melinda and Steve still shake their heads when they recall the Christmas Eve their precious little girl was lost, then miraculously restored. "It didn't seem possible that she'd ever wake up," Melinda says. "But getting her back was the greatest Christmas gift of my life!"

Winter is in my head, but eternal spring
is in my heart.

VICTOR HUGO

A PRISONER'S TALE

BY

EVERETT ALVAREZ, JR., AND
ANTHONY S. PITCH

I had only a moment to think of something to say. It was 1971, and I had been a prisoner of war in North Vietnam for seven long years since my Navy A-4 Skyhawk fighter-bomber was shot down — nightmare years of torture, putrid food and the aching loneliness of frequent solitary confinement. There were almost 400 of us in the infamous prison we had named the Hanoi Hilton.

To combat the monotony, my fellow prisoners had formed a Toastmasters Club. On this particular day I had been given just 30 seconds to prepare a five-minute speech on any personal experience in my life.

Instinctively, my mind whirled back to my family. The adversities we'd faced had shaped my character and given me backbone. My maternal grandmother had married at 13 in Mexico and come to the United States as a railroad man's wife, shunting from one location to another and bedding down in boxcars or tumbledown shacks. My parents had had to drop out of school when they were still children and earn their living. From them I learned about grit, determination and resolve, qualities that had enabled me to survive. More important, I learned about the pure, unquestioning love between parent and child that would surround me forever like a suit of armor.

How could I express all of that? How could I describe for these men the golden treasure given me decades ago by parents so poor? Suddenly I remembered one tiny moment of my childhood, and I knew what I was going to say.

I was eight years old, and we were staying briefly with my grandmother in Salinas, Calif. One day she took me aside and reminded me in a whisper that it was Mom's birthday. I wanted to buy her something nice, but I didn't have any money. There was only one way to scrape some together. I would collect empty soda-pop bottles and trade them in for a penny each at the corner grocery.

With my little red wagon, I foraged for bottles among the neighborhood trash. Each time I filled up the wagon, I trudged to the store.

By late afternoon I figured I had pocketed enough pennies. I pulled my wagon up the hill to the drugstore and brought out my handful of coins. I had enough for a birthday card and even something more.

My eyes locked onto a candy bar. I had just enough money to buy it for Mom. I stuffed the candy in my pants pocket, tucked the card under my shirt and ran home.

By now it was getting dark. As I rounded the corner near our house, I saw Mom looking for me. I could tell she was worried — and angry.

"Where have you been?" she demanded. "I've been searching all over for you!" I was scared, and as she took me inside I started to cry.

"Where were you?" she shouted.

Still blubbering, I explained, "I was out collecting bottles to get money for your birthday present."

I reached into my shirt and gave her the unsigned card. My dirty hands left a smudge where I would have signed it. I then pulled out the candy bar. It had almost snapped in two in my pocket. "I also got you this."

Her anger vanished. She reached out to hug me. As she held me tight and buried her face in my hair, I heard her sobbing. That night, when some neighbors came over, one of them asked why there was a candy bar on the window ledge.

"My son gave that to me as a birthday present," Mom said, proud and moist-eyed.

When I finished telling the story to the P.O.W.s, they sat spellbound. "Damn you, Ev!" one of them finally said as he wiped away tears. I knew then that many of us — the lucky ones — had the same secret treasure of a loving family, the same suit of armor, locked away in a childhood memory. It could see us through the war, no matter how long it took.

Hope is the poor man's bread.

<small>GEORGE HERBERT</small>

A SINGLE CROCUS

BY
JOAN ANDERSON

It was an autumn morning shortly after my husband and I moved into our first house. Our children were upstairs unpacking, and I was looking out the window at my father moving around mysteriously on the front lawn. My parents lived nearby, and Dad had visited us several times already. "What are you doing out there?" I called to him.

He looked up, smiling. "I'm making you a surprise." Knowing my father, I thought it could be just about anything. A self-employed jobber, he was always building things out of odds and ends. When we were kids, he once rigged up a jungle gym out of wheels and pulleys. For one of my Halloween parties, he created an electrical pumpkin and mounted it on a broomstick. As guests came to our door, he would light the pumpkin and have it pop out in front of them from a hiding place in the bushes.

Today, however, Dad would say no more, and, caught up in the busyness of our new life, I eventually forgot about his surprise.

Until one raw day the following March when I glanced out the window. Dismal. Overcast. Little piles of dirty snow still stubbornly littering the lawn. Would winter ever end?

And yet … was it a mirage? I strained to see what I thought was something pink, miraculously peeking out of a drift. And was that a dot of blue across the yard, a small note of optimism in this gloomy expanse? I grabbed my coat and headed outside for a closer look.

They were crocuses, scattered whimsically throughout the front lawn. Lavender, blue, yellow and my favorite pink—little faces bobbing in the bitter wind.

Dad. I smiled, remembering the bulbs he had secretly planted last fall. He knew how the darkness and dreariness of winter always got me down. What could have been more perfectly timed, more attuned to my needs? How blessed I was, not only for the flowers but for him.

My father's crocuses bloomed each spring for the next four or five seasons, bringing that same assurance every time they arrived: *Hard times almost over. Hold on, keep going, light is coming soon.*

Then a spring came with only half the usual blooms. The next spring there were none. I missed the crocuses, but my life was busier than ever, and I had never been much of a gardener. I would ask Dad to come over and plant new bulbs. But I never did.

He died suddenly one October day. My family grieved deeply, leaning on our faith. I missed him terribly, though I knew he would always be a part of us.

Four years passed, and on a dismal spring afternoon I was running errands and found myself feeling depressed. You've got the winter blahs again, I told myself. You get them every year; it's chemistry. But it was something else too.

It was Dad's birthday, and I found myself thinking about him. This was not unusual—my family often talked about him, remembering how he lived his faith. Once I saw him take off his coat and give it to a home-less man. Often he'd chat with strangers passing by his storefront, and if he learned they were poor and hungry, he would invite them home for a meal. But now, in the car, I couldn't help wondering, How is he now? *Where is he?* Is there really a heaven?

I felt guilty for having doubts, but sometimes, I thought as I turned into our driveway, faith is so hard.

Suddenly I slowed, stopped and stared at the lawn. Muddy grass and small gray mounds of melting snow. And there, bravely waving in the wind, was one pink crocus.

How could a flower bloom from a bulb more than 18 years old, one that had not blossomed in over a decade? But there was the crocus. Tears filled my eyes as I realized its significance.

Hold on, keep going, light is coming soon. The pink crocus bloomed for only a day. But it built my faith for a lifetime.

If winter comes, can spring be far behind?

PERCY BYSSHE SHELLEY

A PEARL OF GREAT VALUE

BY
MARCIA EVANS

During my high-school graduation week, 20 of us seniors were summoned by Mr. York, our science teacher, to a mysterious meeting. *Why us?* we wondered.

Mr. York, wearing his signature bow tie and horn-rimmed glasses, handed each of us a small white box.

"Inside," he said, smiling, "you'll find a charm or a tie tack decorated with a seed pearl. Boys and girls, that pearl stands for your potential—the things you have going for you. Just as a seed placed inside an oyster can grow into a pearl of great value, so each of you has a seed of greatness within."

I bit my lip to hold back tears as I stared at the tiny pearl set in a silver charm. How much those words would have meant a day earlier, before I'd learned I was pregnant. The news spelled the end of a dream —my own and my mother's.

As long as I could remember, Mother had set aside a few dollars each week toward college for my sister Marianne and me. Education, she told us, was the way to escape the life of the coal mines in our town of Coaldale, Pa.

I was three when my father entered the sanitarium with tuberculosis. Even after he was released a few years later, Mother's wages from the corner grocery store often fed the family. From hardship was born her dream that one day Marianne and I would change the pattern.

Now, instead of pride, I'd brought shame on the family. In our close-knit Ukrainian Orthodox community, premarital sex was a terrible scandal.

Though we'd wanted to finish college first, Dan and I married after my graduation. By the time Dan graduated from college, a second child had arrived. With a growing family to support, Dan joined the Army. We were moved from base to base, and another child was born. All the while, I'd look at the charm dangling from my wrist and wonder what "greatness" Mr. York had seen in me. Finally, I tucked the bracelet away in a drawer.

After seven years, Dan took a civilian job near Coaldale. Now that our youngest child was in school, I threw myself into volunteer projects. When the restlessness continued, I tried various jobs — store clerk, aerobics instructor.

I was busy, I was helping others, I was adding to the family income, and still — I'd open that drawer, look at the bracelet and think: *Are you building on that little seed Mr. York saw? You have potential. Find it! Use it!* At night, when everyone was asleep, the old goal of college would keep me awake. But then I'd think, *I'm 35 years old!*

My mother must have guessed at my turmoil, because one day on the phone she said, "Remember the college money I saved? It's still there."

I could only stare at the receiver in my hand. Seventeen years had not been enough to blunt Mother's dream. When Mr. York had spoken of "things going for you," I couldn't name one. But now they were everywhere! Faith in God. A mother's dream. A husband's encouragement.

It took me six more months to work up the courage, but in September 1985 I enrolled in Kutztown University. When my aptitude tests pointed to a career in teaching, I was incredulous. Teachers were confident people like Mr. York. But the tests were so definite that I entered the teacher-training program. Going back to school was more difficult than I had feared, however. I was competing with people half my age and feeding my family packaged meals in a dusty house.

One May afternoon that freshman year, after a particularly stressful class, I drove home in tears, wondering if I really belonged back in school. For self-doubters, quitting always seems the sensible thing. Our older daughter would be entering college in the fall. *Instead of straining the family budget,* I thought, *I should be earning money for Kerry's education.*

A few days later, I ran into Mrs. York at the dentist's office. I hadn't seen her in years. I told her about the seed pearl and how it had goaded me back to school. "But it's turning out to be too hard," I said.

"I know," she agreed. "My husband didn't start college till his thirties, either."

I listened, amazed, as she described struggles like my own. I'd always assumed Mr. York had been teaching for years; in fact, I learned that my graduating class had been one of his first. I saw that chance meeting with his wife as a sign that I should stick out the next three years.

After graduating, I took a job teaching English at a local high school. Because of the years I'd spent away from school, I tried to bring the real world into the classroom. Newspapers were as much a part of my curriculum as the classics, factory visits and talks by local employers as important as Shakespeare.

Toward year's end, the principal stunned me by saying he was nominating me for a national award for excellence in first-year teaching. In the application, I was to tell how one of my own teachers had inspired me. And so I told the story of the seed pearl. I realized it had functioned exactly as a seed in an oyster is supposed to—as an irritant, never letting the oyster alone until it's built something beautiful.

In September 1990 I was one of 100 teachers to receive the first-year award, and the teachers who inspired us—including Mr. York—were each given a teacher tribute award. When the two of us met for a newspaper interview, I learned how appropriate the timing was: Mr. York was retiring the following year.

I learned something else that day. My ex-teacher revealed that he, too, had thought he wouldn't succeed. After getting poor grades in high school, he drifted, unable to believe in the future because he didn't believe in himself. What turned him around? "A renewed spirituality and seeing other people's faith in me," he said.

Suddenly, understanding dawned. "That's what we had in common, wasn't it?" I said. "The kids you gave the seed pearls to—you saw 20 young people who lacked confidence."

"No," Mr. York said. "I saw 20 people with seeds of something great."

Hope is brightest when it draws from fears.

SIR WALTER SCOTT

THE POWER OF A NOTE

BY

FRED BAUER

On my first job as sports editor for the Montpelier (Ohio) *Leader Enterprise*, I didn't get a lot of fan mail, so I was intrigued by a letter plopped on my desk one morning. The envelope bore the logo of the closest big-city paper, the Toledo *Blade*.

When I opened it, I read: "Sweet piece of writing on the Tigers. Keep up the good work." It was signed by Don Wolfe, the sports editor. Because I was a teen-ager (being paid the grand total of 15 cents a column inch), his words couldn't have been more exhilarating. I kept the letter in my desk drawer until it got rag-eared. Whenever I doubted I had the right stuff to be a writer, I would reread Don's note and walk on air again.

Later, when I got to know him, I learned that Don made a habit of jotting a quick, encouraging word to people in all walks of life. "When I make others feel good about themselves," he told me, "I feel good too."

Not surprisingly, he had a body of friends as big as nearby Lake Erie. When he died last year at 75, the paper was inundated with calls and letters from people who had been recipients of his spirit-lifting words. Mr. Toledo Blade, as he came to be known, had indeed made them feel good about themselves.

Over the years, I've tried to emulate Don and other friends who care enough to write uplifting comments, because I think they are on to something important. In a world too often cold and unresponsive, such notes are springs of warmth and reassurance. We all need a boost from time to time, and a few lines of praise have been known to turn around a day, even a life.

Why, then, are upbeat note writers in such short supply? My guess is that many who shy away from the practice are too self-conscious. They're afraid they'll be misunderstood, sound corny or fawning. Also, writing takes time; it's far easier to pick up the phone.

The drawback with phone calls, of course, is that they don't last. A note attaches more importance to our well-wishing. It is a matter of record, and our words can be read more than once, savored and treasured.

Even though note writing may take longer, some pretty busy people do it, including George Bush. Some say he owes much of his success in politics to his ever-ready pen. How? Throughout his career he has followed up virtually every contact with a cordial response — a compliment, a line of praise or a nod of thanks. His notes go not only to friends and associates, but to casual acquaintances and total strangers — like the surprised person who got a warm, calligraphic back pat for lending Bush an umbrella.

Even members of the news media, not normally any President's favorite pen pals, have received solicitous notes from the Commander-in-Chief. And so have members of their families. One summer day, when Bush invited some of the press corps to Kennebunkport for a barbecue, the young daughter of Jack Gallivan, a director of ABC's "Primetime Live," went swimming in the Bushes' pool and lost her tooth. Noticing Katie Gallivan crying, Bush asked her what had happened. When he heard, he knew from his own children what that meant: no proof under the pillow for the Tooth Fairy! He called an aide to bring him a Presidential note card bearing an etching of his Kennebunkport house. Bush made a small X on the card and wrote:

Dear Tooth Fairy — Katie's tooth came out where the X is. It really did — I promise.

— *George Bush*

It fulfilled the best prerequisites for inspirational note writing: it was short on verbiage and long on empathy. And most important, it dried Katie's tears.

Another gifted Presidential note writer was Abraham Lincoln. One of his most famous personal letters was a tender condolence to Mrs. Lydia Bixby of Boston, who had lost two sons in battle. "I feel how weak and fruitless must be any words of mine which should attempt to beguile you from the grief of a loss so overwhelming," he wrote. "I pray that our Heavenly Father may assuage the anguish of your bereavement, and leave you only the cherished memory of the loved and lost, and the solemn pride that must be yours to have laid so costly a sacrifice upon the altar of freedom."

Lincoln's wartime letter of loss brings to mind a more recent conflict and some letters of gain. When a New Jersey newspaper urged its subscribers to write to service men and women in Operation Desert Storm, schoolteacher Connie Stanzione accepted the challenge with patriotic fervor. In all, she sent 50 or so letters to anonymous troops.

"I told them how proud I was of them and how much I appreciated their sacrifices for the cause of freedom," she recalls. One who wrote back was 30-year-old Army sergeant Kerry Walters, who thanked Connie for her thoughtfulness. She answered him, and so it went.

Gradually, as they exchanged letters about themselves, they became friends.

After they traded photographs, romance blossomed. Their letters were no longer signed "your friend," but "with love" and "fondly." After a $129 phone call, Kerry sent a letter that concluded: "I pray that I've touched your heart like you have touched mine and that you would like to build a family together. Constance, will you marry me?" Connie immediately accepted. Fittingly, their wedding ceremony included an inspirational message about love from one of the most famous letter writers of all time — St. Paul. His first letter to a small, embattled band of Christians in Corinth so challenged and inspired them that it has been treasured and preserved for 2000 years. I Corinthians 13 tells us that love never ends. And *that* is exactly the power in words of praise.

Even top corporate managers, who have mostly affected styles of leadership that can be characterized only as tough, cold and aloof, have begun to learn the lesson, and earn the benefits, of writing notes that lift people up. Former Ford chairman Donald Petersen, who is largely credited for turning the company around in the 1980s, made it a practice to jot positive messages to associates every day. "I'd just scribble them on a memo pad or the corner of a letter and pass them along," he says. "The most important ten minutes of your day are those you spend doing something to boost the people who work for you."

"Too often," he observed, "people we genuinely like have no idea how we feel about them. Too often we think, *I haven't said anything critical; why do I have to say something positive?* We forget that human beings need positive reinforcement — in fact, we thrive on it!"

What does it take to write letters that lift spirits and warm hearts? Only unselfish eyes and a willingness to express our appreciation. The most successful practitioners include what I call the four "S's" of note writing:

1. *They are sincere.* No one wants their sails filled with smoke.

2. *They are usually short.* If you can't speak your piece in three sentences, you're probably straining.

3. *They are specific.* Complimenting a business colleague by telling him "good speech" is one thing; "great story about Warren Buffet's investment strategy" is another.

4. *They are spontaneous.* This gives them the freshness and enthusiasm that will linger in the reader's mind long afterward.

It's difficult to be spontaneous when you have to hunt for letter-writing materials, so I keep paper, envelopes and stamps close at hand, even when I travel. Fancy stationery isn't necessary; it's the thought that counts.

So, who around you deserves a note of thanks or approval? A neighbor, your librarian, a relative, your mayor, your mate, a teacher, your doctor? You don't need to be poetic. If you need a reason, look for a milestone, the anniversary of a special event you shared, or a birthday or holiday. For the last 25 years, I've prepared an annual Christmas letter for long-distance friends, and I often add a handwritten word of thanks or congratulations. Acknowledging some success or good fortune that has happened during the year seems particularly appropriate considering the spirit of the season.

Don't be stinting with your praise. Superlatives like "greatest," "smartest," "prettiest" — they make us all feel good. Even if your plaudits run a little ahead of reality, remember that expectations are often the parents of dreams fulfilled.

Praise is the best diet

for us all.

SYDNEY SMITH

Today I got a warm, complimentary letter from my old boss and mentor, Norman Vincent Peale. He once told me that the purpose of writing inspirational notes (he is the best three-sentence letter writer I have ever known) is simply "to build others up because there are too many people in the demolition business today."

His little note to me was full of uplifting phrases, and it sent me to my typewriter to compose a few overdue letters of my own. I don't know if they will make anybody else's day, but they made mine. As my friend Don Wolfe said, making others feel good about themselves makes me feel good too.

The most beautiful experience we can have is the mysterious. It is the fundamental emotion which stands at the cradle of true art and true science. Whoever does not know it and can no longer wonder, no longer marvel, is as good as dead, and his eyes are dimmed.

ALBERT EINSTEIN

"I'M HERE TO RENT THE PURPLE FLOWERS"

BY

CHARLES A. HART

One of my granddad's favorite stories was about the farmer who bet that he could lift a full-grown steer. He just wanted 18 months to prove it.

The farmer figured he certainly could pick up a newborn. He expected he could lift it the second day too. Even if the calf gained a few pounds a day, his own strength might grow at an equivalent rate, as long as he kept picking up the calf. So the farmer went out to the corral every morning. As the calf got heavier, the farmer just strained a little harder.

My grandfather never finished this tale. He'd just grin and let listeners draw their own conclusions. He figured the imagination was more powerful than any punch line.

As a child, I bet against the farmer. Common sense says no man can gain strength as fast as a steer gains weight.

On the other hand, why not? Why shouldn't we believe in the impossible? Imagine the farmer, 18 months later, leading a full-grown steer into the corral. As his buddies gape, the farmer hoists the animal and collects his bets.

Today, I like this ending. It suggests that dreams come true and that people are stronger than they think. This interpretation helps me understand my life and the challenge of living with autism.

My attitude about autism began in the 1940s. By age four, I knew my brother, Scott, was our family secret, an embarrassment we sent to a back bedroom when company came.

My sisters and I left home as soon as we could, marrying young or attending college across the country. Scott hadn't chased us away. Fear, shame and confusion had made our home unbearable.

All through my 20s I was plagued by the fear: might I father "a child who never grows up"? But after five years of marriage, I traded my nightmares for hopes, and my wife and I conceived our first child.

At birth, Ted passed every screening, earning a nine out of ten on the newborn scale. But by his second birthday we noticed little quirks. His language was odd. He didn't play with other children. His scores on developmental charts started to slip.

We suffered through a series of diagnoses: brain-damaged, neurologically impaired and, finally, autistic—the same word used to name my brother Scott's problem. We searched for ways to "fix" Ted, but the more we learned, the less we hoped. It looked as though my worst nightmare had come true; my second family seemed as doomed as my first.

On the positive side, my wife and I had resources my parents did not: steady employment, better educations. Medical understanding had progressed. We decided we'd never hide this child. Whether something's a curse or a blessing depends on interpretation. It was up to us.

As my wife and I struggled to understand Ted, we tried not to neglect our second child, born three years later. Raising two sons with such different needs put us to the test. We stumbled through their childhoods until Ted's 21st birthday found us pretty well prepared. He'd graduate at the end of the school year. Between his part-time jobs and a federal assistance check, he'd have a reasonable income. We even fixed up a basement apartment for him.

We thought everything was planned for graduation, but Ted didn't. That spring he caught us off guard with his announcement: "I'm going to the prom." He had thought about it for years. At 18, he'd seen kids his own age plan their prom night. Now Ted saw his chance. All he needed was a date.

He couldn't get a date on his own. Some of the cheerleaders thought he was "cute," but none would actually date him. But a family friend had a daughter, Jennifer. She and Ted had met, they liked each other, and Jennifer understood what prom night meant to him.

We helped Ted prepare, dusting off the etiquette book and the family tuxedo. Ted planned their dinner before the dance. Only one detail remained: the corsage.

It was a very tender symbol, because this young man might never have occasion to present a woman with flowers again. I could have ordered that corsage in two minutes flat. But Ted needed the experience, and I wanted him to have it.

Preparing for the trip to the florist, Ted wanted to role-play. Practicing the words at home makes it easier to say them in another setting. When he had the script down pat, we strolled to our neighborhood florist. But as soon as the little bell on the door stopped jangling, Ted looked trapped. The air was heavy with the smell of flowers. Sachets were everywhere.

The clerk, hearing the door, turned to us. Ted cleared his throat. He drew his face into a grimace and blurted out, "I'm Ted. I'm here to rent the purple flowers."

The clerk looked startled. Ted furrowed his brows. "Look at her," I suggested, "and tell her what you want to order."

Finally, by staying calm and speaking slowly, he answered the clerk's questions. He wanted a corsage for Saturday. His date wanted to wear it on her wrist. He preferred purple or lavender roses. He'd pay when he picked it up.

This conversation would have been easy for most people. But unfamiliar environments make Ted nervous. After 21 years, I had grown accustomed to Ted's responses. Still, I hadn't expected the clerk's reaction.

"You have a lot of patience," she said to me. "I could never be so patient."

Her initial bewilderment had changed to sympathy, then to admiration. But she was admiring the wrong person. Unknown to the clerk, my son had climbed mountains of barriers and swum oceans of confusion just to reach this point. Saturday night wouldn't find him working a jigsaw puzzle as his uncle had spent his youth. Ted was going to the prom!

No! I wanted to shout. *I'm not patient.* My nervous system works. It transmits signals instantaneously from memory bank to nerve center to vocal cords and back. Ted, though, has to labor these pathways, struggling upstream toward a life the rest of us take for granted.

Prom night I dropped Ted and Jennifer at the dance. At home I called one of my sisters. We talked about our brother's stunted life and the amazing progress Ted had already made. We cried.

Today I keep a photo from the dance on my desk. Jennifer stands beside Ted. On her wrist she wears a corsage of lavender roses. That image freezes in time.

Before I knew he faced special challenges, I had typical ambitions for my son. I hoped my children would be better, more successful versions of my wife and me. I couldn't predict that he'd wrench me from the mainstream and lead me in a more interesting direction.

When my son was very young, he was easy to lift. It seemed appropriate to make decisions for him—choosing clothes, scheduling activities. It's harder now. Not because Ted's heavier. My *conscience* is heavier. He is as entitled to freedom of choice and expression as I am. So whenever I try to influence him, I'd better be certain it's for his best interest, not my peace of mind.

Twenty years ago I didn't think I could cope with a son's disability. It had never occurred to me that I could become a stronger person, that I would discover meaning and direction for my own life through the challenge of another person.

I hadn't done anything extraordinary, just lifted my calf each day. Grandpa was right not to finish the story. We write our own endings.

Our highest assurance of the goodness of providence rests in the flowers. All other things—our powers, our desires, our food—are necessary for our existence, but the rose is an extra. Its smell and its color are an embellishment of life, not a condition of it. It is only goodness which gives extras, and so we have much to hope from the flowers.

SIR ARTHUR CONAN DOYLE

THE DAY AT THE BEACH

BY

ARTHUR GORDON

Not long ago I came to one of those bleak periods that many of us encounter from time to time, a sudden drastic dip in the graph of living when everything goes stale and flat, energy wanes, enthusiasm dies. The effect on my work was frightening. Every morning I would clench my teeth and mutter: "Today life will take on some of its old meaning. You've got to break through this thing. You've got to!"

But the barren days went by, and the paralysis grew worse. The time came when I knew I had to have help.

The man I turned to was a doctor. Not a psychiatrist, just a doctor. He was older than I, and under his surface gruffness lay great wisdom and compassion. "I don't know what's wrong," I told him miserably, "but I just seem to have come to a dead end. Can you help me?"

"I don't know," he said slowly. He made a tent of his fingers, and gazed at me thoughtfully for a long while. Then, abruptly, he asked, "Where were you happiest as a child?"

"As a child?" I echoed. "Why, at the beach, I suppose. We had a summer cottage there. We all loved it."

He looked out the window and watched the October leaves sifting down. "Are you capable of following instructions for a single day?"

"I think so," I said, ready to try anything.

"All right. Here's what I want you to do."

He told me to drive to the beach alone the following morning, arriving not later than nine o'clock. I could take some lunch, but I was not to read, write, listen to the radio or talk to anyone. "In addition," he said, "I'll give you a prescription to be taken every three hours."

He tore off four prescription blanks, wrote a few words on each, folded them, numbered them and handed them to me. "Take these at nine, twelve, three and six."

"Are you serious?" I asked.

He gave a short bark of a laugh. "You won't think I'm joking when you get my bill!"

The next morning, with little faith, I drove to the beach. It was lonely, all right. A northeaster was blowing; the sea looked gray and angry. I sat in the car, the whole day stretching emptily before me. Then I took out the first of the folded slips of paper. On it was written: *Listen carefully.*

I stared at the two words. Why, I thought, the man must be mad. He had ruled out music and newscasts and human conversation. What else was there?

I raised my head and I did listen. There were no sounds but the steady roar of the sea, the creaking cry of a gull, the drone of some aircraft high overhead. All these sounds were familiar.

I got out of the car. A gust of wind slammed the door with a sudden clap of sound. Am I supposed, I asked myself, to listen carefully to things like that?

I climbed a dune and looked out over the deserted beach. Here the sea bellowed so loudly that all other sounds were lost. And yet, I thought suddenly, there must be sounds beneath sounds — the soft rasp of drifting sand, the tiny wind-whisperings in the dune grasses — if the listener got close enough to hear them.

On an impulse I ducked down and feeling faintly ridiculous, thrust my head into a clump of sea-wheat. Here I made a discovery: if you listen intently, there is a fractional moment in which everything seems to pause, wait. In that instant of stillness, the racing thoughts halt. For a moment, when you truly listen for something outside yourself, you have to silence the clamorous voices within. The mind rests.

I went back to the car and slid behind the wheel. *Listen carefully.* As I listened again to the deep growl of the sea, I found myself thinking about the immensity of it, the stupendous rhythms of it, the velvet trap it made for moonlight, the white-fanged fury of its storms.

I thought of the lessons it had taught us as children. A certain amount of patience: you can't hurry the tides. A great deal of respect: the sea does not suffer fools gladly. An awareness of the vast mysterious interdependence of things: wind and tide and current, calm and squall and hurricane, all combining to determine the paths of the birds above and the fish below. And the cleanness of it all, with every beach swept twice a day by the great broom of the sea.

Sitting there, I realized I was thinking of things bigger than myself — and there was relief in that.

Even so, the morning passed slowly. The habit of hurling myself at a problem was so strong that I felt lost without it. Once, when I was wistfully eyeing the car radio, a phrase from Carlyle jumped into my head: "Silence is the element in which great things fashion themselves . . ."

By noon the wind had polished the clouds out of the sky, and the sea had a hard, merry sparkle. I unfolded the second "prescription." And again I sat there, half amused and half exasperated. Three words this time: *Try reaching back.*

Back to what? To the past, obviously. Buy why, when all my worries concerned the present or the future?

I left the car and started tramping reflectively along the dunes. The doctor had sent me to the beach because it was a place of happy memories. Maybe *that* was what I was supposed to reach for: the wealth of happiness that lay half-forgotten behind me.

I found a sheltered place and lay down on the sun-warmed sand. When I tried to peer into the well of the past, the recollections that came to the surface were happy but not very clear; the faces were faint and faraway, as if I had not thought of them in a long time.

I decided to experiment: to work on these vague impressions as a painter would, retouching the colors, strengthening the outlines. I would choose specific incidents and recapture as many details as possible. I would visualize people complete with dress and gestures. I would listen (carefully!) for the exact sound of their voices, the echo of their laughter.

The tide was going out now, but there was still thunder in the surf. So I chose to go back 20 years to the last fishing trip I made with my younger brother. (He died in the Pacific during World War II, and was buried in the Philippines.) I found now that if I closed my eyes and really tried I could see him with amazing vividness, even the humor and eagerness in his eyes that far-off morning.

In fact, I could see it all: the ivory scimitar of beach where we were fishing, the eastern sky smeared with sunrise, the great rollers creaming in, stately and slow. I could feel the backwash swirl warm around my knees, see the sudden arc of my brother's rod as he struck a fish, hear his exultant yell. Piece by piece I rebuilt it, clear and unchanged under the transparent varnish of time. Then it was gone.

I sat up slowly. *Try reaching back.* Happy people were usually assured, confident people. If, then, you deliberately reached back and touched happiness, might there not be released little flashes of power, tiny sources of strength?

This second period of the day went more quickly. As the sun began its long slant down the sky, my mind ranged eagerly through the past, reliving some episodes, uncovering others that had been completely forgotten. For example, when I was around 13 and my brother 10, Father had promised to take us to the circus. But at lunch there was a phone call: some urgent business required his attention downtown. We braced ourselves for disappointment. Then we heard him say, "No, I won't be down. It'll have to wait."

When he came back to the table, Mother smiled. "The circus keeps coming back, you know."

"I know," said Father. "But childhood doesn't."

Across all the years I remembered this, and knew from the sudden glow of warmth that no kindness is ever really wasted, or ever completely lost.

By three o'clock the tide was out; the sound of the waves was only a rhythmic whisper, like a giant breathing. I stayed in my sandy nest, feeling relaxed and content — and a little complacent. The doctor's prescriptions, I thought, were easy to take.

But I was not prepared for the next one. This time the three words were not a gentle suggestion. They sounded more like a command. *Re-examine your motives.*

My first reaction was purely defensive. there's nothing wrong with my motives, I said to myself. I want to be successful — who doesn't? I want a certain amount of recognition — but so does everybody. I want more security than I've got — and why not?

Maybe, said a small voice somewhere inside my head, those motives aren't good enough. Maybe that's the reason the wheels have stopped going round.

I picked up a handful of sand and let it stream between my fingers. In the past, whenever my work went well, there had always been something spontaneous about it, something uncontrived, something free. Lately it had been calculated, competent — and dead. Why? Because I had been looking past the job itself to the rewards I hoped it would bring. The work had ceased to be an end in itself; it had been merely a means to make money, pay bills. The sense of *giving* something, of helping people, of making a contribution, had been lost in a frantic clutch at security.

In a flash of certainty, I saw that if one's motives are wrong, nothing can be right. It makes no difference whether you are a mailman, a hair-dresser, an insurance salesman, a housewife — whatever. As long as you feel you are serving others, you do the job well. When you are concerned only with helping yourself, you do it less well. This is a law as inexorable as gravity.

For a long time I sat there. Far out on the bar I heard the murmur of the surf change to a hollow roar as the tide turned. Behind me the spears of light were almost horizontal. My time at the beach had almost run out, and I felt a grudging admiration for the doctor and the "prescriptions" he had so casually and cunningly devised. I saw, now, that in them was a therapeutic progression that might well be of value to anyone facing any difficulty.

Listen carefully: To calm the frantic mind, slow it down, shift the focus from inner problems to outer things.

Try reaching back: Since the human mind can hold but one idea at a time, you blot out present worry when you touch the happinesses of the past.

Men go forth to wonder at the height of mountains, the huge waves of the sea — and forget to wonder at themselves.

ST. AUGUSTINE

Re-examine your motives: This was the hard core of the "treatment," this challenge to reappraise, to bring one's motives into alignment with one's capabilities and conscience. But the mind must be clear and receptive to do this — hence the six hours of quiet that went before.

The western sky was a blaze of crimson as I took out the last slip of paper. Six words this time. I walked slowly out on the beach. A few yards below high-water mark I stopped and read the words again: *Write your worries on the sand.*

I let the paper blow away, reached down and picked up a fragment of shell. Kneeling there under the vault of the sky, I wrote several words on the sand, one above the other.

Then I walked away, and I did not look back. I had written my troubles on the sand. And the tide was coming in.

Hope, like the gleaming taper's light,

Adorns and cheers our way;

And still, as darker grows the night,

Emits a brighter ray.

OLIVER GOLDSMITH

OUR SNOW NIGHT

BY

JAMES TABOR

It comes every winter, this one perfect night. The air is clear and still, snow squeaks underfoot, and the full moon rises like a great golden balloon over the small, snow-draped mountain behind our Vermont house. All around us, the snowfields gleam like polished silver.

My wife puts a kettle of hot cocoa on the wood stove, for later. We bundle in snow boots and layers of red wool. Outside, the air nips at noses and cheeks as we strap on our snowshoes. When everyone's ready, we set off through the white-birch grove behind our house. The trunks, straight as pillars, shine like ice in the moonlight. Our teen-age son strides out first, making the trail.

This light — this incredible, blue-white, twice-reflected light! Surely it is the gentlest, most beautiful light on earth. It softens everything — faces, voices, even thoughts. It twinkles on icicles dangling from branch tips, gleams on rounded drifts. Slipping single file through the woods, we trail tight puffs of breath and feel the snow compress beneath our wide wooden paws. After a while, we spy the heart-shaped tracks of deer.

My wife tosses up a handful of snow, and the crystals hang suspended, sparkling like stars. The flakes tickle our four-year-old's cheeks and he laughs, a silvery sound here, like harp chords. These woods are enchanted, the world under a spell. Three hundred years ago, Abnaki Indians traveled here on white-ash snowshoes like ours. We feel the power of the secrets they knew.

Fifteen minutes brings us to the meadow. It spreads before us, a quarter-mile of purest white, smooth as taut satin. We fan out, eager to make new tracks. Our movements reveal us, distinctive as signatures. The teen-ager is a natural, slicing along like a skater. His little brother churns, with head down and arms pumping, spraying a fluffy wake. My wife, light as a cat, barely ruffles the snow. I stroke along, finding my pace. Swing and plant, swing and plant. My lungs pull in great drafts of the cold, pure air.

At the meadow's far edge we enter a maple grove and start to climb. Low gear, here — short steps, staying just this side of sweat. My wife turns and grins, as she always does on this hillside, and I smile back.

Thirty minutes and we're on top of the knob that protects our house from northern winds. We halt in a clearing, cooling after the climb. The muscles in the backs of my legs and chest are warm but not burned. My brain, supercharged with cold oxygen, is almost giddy.

Treats emerge from my wife's pack — Christmas candy canes, dried apricots, almonds — and we sit on a log, refueling. New energy blows through us like a refreshing wind.

Below, the village spreads out, windows glowing orange. Smoke curls from chimneys in silver ribbons. Our youngest calls out the names of friends and neighbors below us.

My wife takes my mittened hand while our boys toss snowballs to the moon. Soon we'll head home to the cocoa, downhilling on our shoes — the ultimate fun, like wading through clouds.

But not yet. For now, in this fusion of light, we ourselves are aglow. We know what the Abnaki knew, what the deer know, and the breeze and streams. We know the secret: we *are* the secret. We are a family.

Behind the cloud the starlight lurks,

    Through showers the sunbeams fall;

For God, who loveth all his works,

    Has left his Hope with all.

JOHN GREENLEAF WHITTIER

SEASON OF MIRACLES

BY

JOHN PEKKANEN

*A*s they listened to a recording of "The Star-Spangled Banner," 12 young ballplayers anxiously awaited the opening game of junior baseball in North Charleston, S.C. Feelings ran high among the seven- and eight-year-olds, members of the Steve Evans Reds.

One of the Reds, Jason Ellis "E. J." Fludd, eight, hovered near third-base coach Sandra Evans. "Aunt Sandy," E. J. asked searchingly, "is Coach Stevie up there watching us?"

Sandy, 32, answered softly. "Yes, E. J. I think Steve's spirit is right here with us."

"Play ball!" the umpire shouted. Sandy, tears welling, watched her team dash onto the field. *This season is for you, Steve,* she thought, as her mind drifted back to a year earlier.

"Sandy, we have a dinner guest," Steve Evans called out as he strolled in the front door. Just home from baseball practice, Steve had with him a shy, black youngster the players all called E.J.

Steve always had a soft spot for kids. An easygoing 34-year-old with reddish hair and a lanky frame, he had volunteered to coach the team. In the early spring of 1991, he'd rush home from his job as an insulation installer to get to the practice field. Patient and encouraging, Steve proved an ideal coach for the restless, diverse group of youngsters—some white, some black, others Asian. "Several come from troubled backgrounds," he told Sandy. "I'm coaching to help them feel better about themselves."

One boy, E.J., laughed harder—and played harder—than all the others. He lived with his mother, who worked long hours as a cook at the Charleston Air Force Base. Having little contact with his father, E. J. was lonely much of the time. After every practice, he would give Steve a bear hug and say, "Thanks, Coach Stevie."

At dinner that first evening, E.J. won over the entire family. Soon he was coming regularly for dinner, often staying overnight. Sandy became "Aunt Sandy." Steve would include E. J. in family softball games with his son Timmy, 12, daughter Stephanie, ten, and four nephews—Thomas, Steven and David Evans, and James Garvin. The four nephews played with E. J. on the team.

The only bad news that year was at the ballpark—where Steve's team lost game after game. E. J. would slump in dejection at every defeat, or when he made an error.

During one losing game, Steve put an arm around the boy. "Hold your head up, E. J.," he said. "You don't have anything to be ashamed of."

Steve then pulled out an Atlanta Braves baseball card. "See this?" he asked. "One day your picture will be on one of these."

E.J.'s eyes lit up. "You mean I could play for the Braves someday?"

"Sure, as long as you keep working hard and don't give up. You shouldn't ever give up on anything."

Then, on June 17, 1991, an uncle of Steve's told Sandy there had been an explosion at a chemical plant, where Steve was working that day. After a dozen fruitless phone calls to area hospitals, Sandy heard the crushing news from Steve's employer; Steve had been killed when a chemical reactor exploded. Sandy slumped to the floor, all feeling draining out of her.

Sandy was 17, just out of high school, when she married Steve in 1976. They'd both grown up in modest neighborhoods. Once, while they were dating, the washing machine owned by Sandy's family broke down, and there was no money to buy a new one. Steve found a beat-up washer, fixed it, then gave it to Sandy's family. The thoughtfulness left Sandy stunned.

After Steve and Sandy were married, money remained tight—but they still had fun. Steve loved driving Sandy and the children to Florida's Disney World, or spending a day "tubing" on nearby lakes and rivers.

Now Sandy sat in the funeral home, numb with grief. Looking up, she saw Steve's team, in their uniforms, file slowly in. A few moments later, Sandy noticed E. J., tears pouring down his cheeks, as he sat with his mother.

"He hasn't stopped crying since Steve died," E. J.'s mother said. Sandy opened her arms wide, and E. J. climbed into her lap. As he wept, Sandy held his trembling body close, trying to give him the comfort she couldn't give herself.

After Steve's funeral, the team played its remaining games in a daze. They lost them all.

In the following months, Sandy's sister, Louann Ackerman, grew increasingly worried. Sandy was sinking deeper and deeper into her private grief. When her sister stopped eating and lost 40 pounds, Louann felt panic. "This may be her way of ending it all," she said to her husband, Ira.

Then early in 1992, Louann had an idea. "In Steve's memory," she told Sandy, "I want to sponsor this year's team for you."

"Funny," Sandy said, "I'd been thinking I might sponsor the team myself as a way to honor Steve. He loved those kids." Sandy and Louann renamed the team the Steve Evans Reds, for Steve's red hair. When Sandy told E. J., he said, "I promise you, Aunt Sandy, we're gonna win all our games for Coach Stevie." Steve's friend, Ron Gadsden, agreed to become coach and continue as manager.

On a warm March afternoon, the Reds gathered for their first practice. Forming the nucleus of the team were E. J., Sandy's four nephews, and Ron Gadsden's son, Ryan. Because some of the previous season's players were over the age limit, new ones were added. Younger and smaller than the ones they replaced, some of the new boys had no idea how to catch or hit. *This is going to be a rough season,* Louann thought.

Coach Gadsden drilled the new kids on how to hold a bat and swing. E. J. coached them on the man that the team was named for. "Coach Stevie took a lot of time with us," E. J. explained, his voice cracking. "He was always nice, and he made us laugh." Then E. J. told the team, "We've got to win this year for Coach Stevie." Slowly, the message sank in, as the Reds approached their opening day on April 11.

Today, well lived, makes every yesterday a dream of happiness and every tomorrow a vision of hope.

SANSKRIT PROVERB

In the first inning of the season's first game, the Charleston Apartments Giants took a quick two-run lead before the Reds came to bat. E. J. hit a home run to lead a four-run counterattack. By the bottom half of the final inning, the score was tied 8-8. Then Thomas Evans hit a home run. To everyone's surprise, the Reds had won.

When the Reds won again, Louann noticed changes in her sister. During the games Sandy, leaden and unemotional after Steve's death, started clapping and shouting. By the time the Reds won their third game, she had begun eating again.

"With this team," Sandy told Louann, "I feel that Steve's not gone completely. There's a piece of him still here with all of us."

The team was also changing. The youngsters began saying, "We can't be beat!" Sandy, worried that E. J. and her nephews were feeling too much pressure to win for Steve, called them aside. "Remember," she said, "it's just a game."

"You don't understand, Aunt Sandy," E. J. said earnestly. "We *have* to win for Coach Stevie!"

Sandy turned away, fighting back tears. *If we ever lose,* she thought, *these kids'll be shattered.*

As the season entered May, the Reds kept on rolling. They took one game 16-7 and another 17-6.

Sandy drew strength from E. J. *Just look at this little boy,* she thought. *He's hurting so much, yet he's still so loving and joyful.* Slowly, Sandy began looking forward to the games and practices with a gladness she once feared she'd never feel again. Now when a game ended, she took the team for pizzas. She even found herself laughing out loud.

"It's a miracle we're winning," Louann told her husband after another Reds victory. "But the real miracle is seeing E. J. help Sandy to heal. I'm getting my sister back."

Near the end of the season, the undefeated Reds stood at the top of the league. To win the championship they had to beat the Giants—the team the Reds had defeated by only one run on opening day. That game stood as the Giants' only loss.

The day of the final game, May 23, the temperature soared into the 90s. The Giants took an early lead in the first inning with four runs. The Reds fought back, and by the end of the second inning, the two teams were tied 4-4. Then the Giants went on a hitting spree and moved ahead 10-4. This was the first time all season that the Reds had been so far behind. "Come on, we can still win," E. J. shouted to his teammates.

However, the tension became too much for Thomas Evans, and he suddenly burst into tears. Sandy raced out and pulled him close. "It's okay," she whispered.

"We're gonna lose, Aunt Sandy!" Thomas said.

"Don't worry about losing," she assured him. "We've done our best, so it's all right."

Although the Reds reduced the Giants' lead, they couldn't catch up. The Giants went ahead 12-9 with one inning to go.

The Reds trotted off the field for their last time at bat. Suddenly, Thomas Evans knelt near the pitcher's mound, drawing in the red dirt with his finger, then walked silently toward the dugout. On the mound he'd written his uncle's name.

"I wanted Uncle Steve to know we were thinking about him," Thomas told Sandy. Word of what the boy had done spread quickly through the Reds' dugout. Moments later, however, reality set in. The Reds had two runners on base—but there were now two outs. The dugout went silent.

The Reds' last hope was David Evans, the smallest player on the team. As he walked toward the plate, Louann prayed silently. *Dear Lord, please, help these kids. And Sandy.*

David, not much taller than his bat, made up for his small size with a scrappy attitude. On the first pitch, he swung awkwardly and missed. Then he fouled off another pitch. *It's finally over,* Sandy thought sadly to herself.

With the next pitch, David made contact, but the ball headed in the worst possible direction—straight toward first base and the best player on the Giants' team. Coach Gadsden, figuring the game was over, began walking toward the Reds' dugout.

The Giants' first baseman reached down to scoop up the ball—but it squirted past him.

David raced to second base as one run scored. This cut the Giants' lead to two, and there were runners on second and third.

Thomas Evans, next at bat, sent the ball flying for a clean hit. Sandy waved two runners home. With the game now tied, the Reds and their fans traded high-fives.

The next batter, Ryan Gadsden, got another hit, and by the time E. J. got to the plate, there were three runners on base. On the second pitch, E. J. connected perfectly, and the ball sailed deep into right-center field—a grand slam.

His teammates mobbed him. Sandy jumped up and down in the coach's box.

The Reds now led for the first time in the game, and more hits followed. When the third out finally came, the Reds had pushed across 11 runs in all. "I've seen it, but I can't believe it," Louann yelled when Sandy returned to the dugout.

Disheartened and exhausted, the Giants went down without scoring. The Reds had won the league championship, 20-12. That night, E. J. went to sleep clutching his player trophy for the championship.

Eight days later, Sandy stood at Steve's graveside with E. J. and her four nephews. The date—May 31—would have been Steve's 36th birthday.

Sandy knelt and, on her husband's grave, placed a photograph of the Reds holding their team trophy. The picture was signed by all the players and coaches. "The team won the championship for you, Steve," Sandy said softly. "And we know you helped them do it."

She held a small figurine dressed in a baseball uniform with "Number 1 Coach" written on it. She placed the figurine on the grave. *I'll always remember you, Coach Stevie,* E. J. thought.

Then they all joined hands and prayed. A few moments later, they walked silently away.

There was never a night or a problem that could

defeat sunrise or hope.

BERN WILLIAMS

TEARDROPS OF HOPE

BY

NANCY SULLIVAN GENG

My friend Lauri and I had brought our kids to the park that day to celebrate my 35th birthday. From a picnic table we watched them laugh and leap through the playground while we unpacked a basket bulging with sandwiches and cookies.

We toasted our friendship with bottles of mineral water. It was then that I noticed Lauri's new drop earrings. In the 13 years I'd known Lauri, she'd always loved drop earrings. I'd seen her wear pair after pair: threaded crystals cast in blue, strands of colored gemstones, beaded pearls in pastel pink.

"There's a reason why I like drop earrings," Lauri told me.

She began revealing images of a childhood that changed her forever, a tale of truth and its power to transform.

It was a spring day. Lauri was in sixth grade, and her classroom was cheerfully decorated. Yellow May Day baskets hung suspended on clotheslines above desks, caged hamsters rustled in shredded newspaper and orange marigolds curled over cutoff milk cartons on window shelves.

The teacher, Mrs. Lake, stood in front of the class, her auburn hair flipping onto her shoulders like Jackie Kennedy's, her kind, blue eyes sparkling. But it was her drop earrings that Lauri noticed most—golden teardrop strands laced with ivory pearls. "Even from my back-row seat," Lauri recalled, "I could see those earrings gleaming in the sunlight from the windows."

Mrs. Lake reminded the class it was the day set aside for end-of-the-year conferences. Both parents and students would participate in these important progress reports. On the blackboard, an alphabetical schedule assigned 20 minutes for each family.

Lauri's name was at the end of the list. But it didn't matter much. Despite at least one reminder letter mailed home and the phone calls her teacher had made, Lauri knew her parents would not be coming.

Lauri's father was an alcoholic, and that year his drinking had escalated. Many nights Lauri would fall asleep hearing the loud, slurred voice of her father, her mother's sobs, slamming doors, pictures rattling on the wall.

The previous Christmas Lauri and her sister had saved baby-sitting money to buy their dad a shoeshine kit. They had wrapped the gift with red-and-green paper and trimmed it with a gold ribbon curled into a bow. When they gave it to him on Christmas Eve, Lauri watched in stunned silence as he threw it across the living room, breaking it into three pieces.

Now Lauri watched all day long as each child was escorted to the door leading into the hallway, where parents would greet their sons or daughters with proud smiles, pats on the back and sometimes even hugs. The door would close, and Lauri would try to distract herself with her assignments. But she couldn't help hearing the muffled voices as parents asked questions, children giggled nervously and Mrs. Lake spoke. Lauri imagined how it might feel to have her parents greet her at the door.

When at last everyone else's name had been called, Mrs. Lake opened the door and motioned for Lauri. Silently Lauri slipped out into the hallway and sat down on a folding chair. Across from the chair was a desk covered with student files and projects. Curiously she watched as Mrs. Lake looked through the files and smiled.

Embarrassed that her parents had not come, Lauri folded her hands and looked down at the linoleum. Moving her desk chair next to the downcast little girl, Mrs. Lake lifted Lauri's chin so she could make eye contact. "First of all," the teacher began, "I want you to know how much I love you."

Lauri lifted her eyes. In Mrs. Lake's face she saw things she'd rarely seen: compassion, empathy, tenderness.

"Second," the teacher continued, "you need to know it is not your fault that your parents are not here today."

Again Lauri looked into Mrs. Lake's face. No one had ever talked to her like this. No one.

"Third," she went on, "you deserve a conference whether your parents are here or not. You deserve to hear how well you are doing and how wonderful I think you are."

In the following minutes, Mrs. Lake held a conference just for Lauri. She showed Lauri her grades. She scanned Lauri's papers and projects, praising her efforts and affirming her strengths. She had even saved a stack of watercolors Lauri had painted.

Lauri didn't know exactly when, but at some point in that conference she heard the voice of hope in her heart. And somewhere a transformation started.

As tears welled in Lauri's eyes, Mrs. Lake's face became misty and hazy—except for her drop earrings of golden curls and ivory pearls. What were once irritating intruders in oyster shells had been transformed into things of beauty.

It was then that Lauri realized, for the first time in her life, that she was lovable.

As we sat together in a comforting silence, I thought of all the times Lauri had worn the drop earrings of truth for me.

All my life I had fought off feelings of insecurity; memories from the past always whispering: you're less than loveable. But Lauri had met me in a symbolic hallway of empathy. There she helped me see that the shimmering jewel of self-worth is a gift from God that everyone deserves. She showed me that even adulthood is not too late to don the dazzling diamonds of new-found self-esteem.

Just then the kids ran up and flopped onto the grass to dramatize their hunger. For the rest of the afternoon we wiped spilled milk, praised off-balance somersaults and glided down slides much too small for us.

But in the midst of it all, Lauri handed me a small box, a birthday gift wrapped in red floral paper trimmed with a gold bow.

I opened it. Inside was a pair of drop earrings.

The natural flights of the human mind
are not from pleasure to pleasure but
from hope to hope.

SAMUEL JOHNSON

BRINGING UP
BUTTERCUP

BY

PENNY PORTER

"Where were you?" Bill hung his weathered Stetson on the bull-horn rack by the wood stove and fixed his eyes on our 12-year-old daughter.

Becky, deep in an algebra assignment at the kitchen table, didn't look up. "I couldn't come out and help, Daddy," she said. "I get extra credit if I do these equations."

Her father ruffled her honey-blond hair. "Well, we sure could have used an extra hand on that corral gate. Then those cows wouldn't have broken through the darn fence."

His tone was gentle, but I knew he was concerned about Becky. She was too much like he used to be. Bill had been a math whiz himself, earning an engineering degree and planning a lucrative career. But his time as a P.O.W. during World War II changed his thinking. Back home, he chose to be an Arizona rancher. He could spend more time doing what he now considered important—drawing closer to his family and the land. In particular, Bill enjoyed animals and wanted his children to share that experience.

Two of our older children, Bud and Scott, showed bulls and heifers at county fairs. Our youngest, Jaymee, could hardly wait to do the same. But Becky loved numbers.

Bill, however, refused to give up. "Wouldn't you like to show your very own yearling heifer next year?" he asked Becky one day. "You could win a blue ribbon!"

"I'm too busy, Daddy. I've got tests coming up. And I help other kids in math."

"Come on, honey. I'll give you the calf out of my best cow. When it's ready to show, you can sell it and keep the money for college." Reluctantly Becky followed Bill into his office. He sifted through pedigree notebooks that listed dozens of names, each identified with eight-digit numbers. "Here she is! Tag 333. Look at the bloodlines! Her baby will be one heck of a calf!"

Becky looked, and a smile brightened her face. I understood. It was all those numbers beneath Tag 333's name and under the ancestors. "Okay, Daddy. I'll give it a try."

In the following weeks, she started a journal of projected expenses—vaccinations, registration fees, vet bills, grain and hay. "She's finally getting interested in cattle," Bill told me happily.

I wasn't so sure. For Becky, the calf seemed more like a mathematical challenge than a living animal that would require care and love.

Something else gnawed at me. Unlike most Herefords, Tag 333 was a crazy thing with wild eyes, flaring nostrils and horns like grappling hooks. She soared over fences into neighbors' pastures and bolted into chutes backward and flipped over. "Aren't you worried that cow might reject her baby?" I asked Bill.

"Her mama had six calves and no problems," he replied. "It's all in the genes."

One February night, as we climbed into bed, Bill said, "Tag 333's due to calve any time now."

"Well, let's hope she doesn't have it tonight," I replied. "It's supposed to get *really* cold."

In the morning, Bill called, "Come see this! I'll bet it's well below zero out there."

Winter's magic had transformed our pastures into a wonderland. Icicles clung like strings of festive lights along miles of irrigation pipes. Cattle huddled in bunches, steam rising like wood smoke from their broad backs. Calves shivered at their mothers' sides. Calves! My heart leapt. "What about Tag 333?" I asked Bill.

He frowned. "We can't find her. Scott's checking the other pastures."

I lit the wood stove and woke Becky and Jaymee for school. They were eating breakfast when 22-year-old Scott burst in. "Can't locate that cow, Dad. But I saw her calf about two miles down. It's in bad shape. You better bring the truck."

Piling into the pickup, we drove to where the newborn lay glazed in ice. Her eyelids were sealed by glittering frost. Scott began knocking away the icicles imprisoning the rigid body. "It's a little heifer," he murmured.

"Is she dead?" Becky asked.

Scott pressed his fingers against the calf's chest. "No heartbeat, Dad."

"Let's get her to the barn—fast!" Bill and Scott gripped her legs and pried the 70-pound calf from the earth, swinging her into the truck. She struck the metal bed like a slab of granite.

"She's frozen solid!" gasped Scott, jumping in beside the calf. To get her circulation going, he began rubbing her with a burlap sack. The rest of us climbed into the pickup. "Oh no!" Becky cried. Ahead she saw brown and white chunks of fur where the calf had been. "We left pieces of her ears behind!" she wailed.

In the straw-filled stall, the calf lay motionless. Bill thumped and squeezed the calf as Scott searched for a vein to insert an I.V. Becky watched. "What can I do, Daddy?"

"Get some blankets to warm her."

Scott gave a whoop. "We've got a heartbeat!"

I hurried to the house for colostrum, "first milk" that we keep for emergencies. A few drops in the calf's mouth and the tiny jaws moved slightly. Soon the tug on the bottle told me she was nursing.

"You're going to be all right," Becky whispered as she stroked the calf's cold face.

But Bill, Scott and I knew the dangers, even if the calf survived: pneumonia, kidney damage, arthritis. "Becky, if she doesn't make it," Bill said, "I'll help you pick another calf."

"I don't want another one, Daddy. Besides, I've already named her—Buttercup." The unexpected emotion in Becky's voice startled us.

The calf was in a deep sleep. Scott hung the I.V. from a rafter. "Can I stay with her?" Becky asked. "She might wiggle out from the covers." When I checked later, Becky and Buttercup were both under the blankets.

After lunch, Scott removed the I.V. The calf was shivering violently by now. Becky gave her a bottle. At the four o'clock feeding, the calf's brown eyes were bright with anticipation. "Look!" Becky said. "She knows me!"

Eager to nurse, the little creature struggled to stand, but her legs were still jackknifed beneath her. All she could do was flop around. Then she'd look at Becky and bawl.

The next morning I found the calf buttoned into one of Bill's old sweaters. *Becky,* I quickly realized.

Hope has as many lives

as a cat or a king.

HENRY WADSWORTH LONGFELLOW

"How'd you get her legs through those sleeves?" I asked.

"She let me straighten them, and after a while they'll stay straight, Mama. I know they will." But straw and blankets were tossed everywhere—evidence of the calf's all-night battle to stand. *Please,* I prayed, *don't let my daughter get too attached.*

We were leaving for the school bus when Bill spoke softly to Scott. "We'll take care of that calf." Becky knew what that meant. But as I drove her to the bus stop, she said, "Daddy will think of something."

When I got home, Bill and Scott were heading to the barn. I turned up the radio to drown out the crack of the rifle. After an hour I went to check. "Steady, girl," I heard Bill say. I looked into the stall. The calf's legs were wrapped in cotton batting and splints made from plastic pipe. Buttercup was standing!

By the end of the day, Buttercup was walking. After school, Becky put a halter on her, and they toured the barnyard. Two weeks later, Scott removed the splints. Although her knees still trembled and swelled, Buttercup continued to walk. But now her fight against respiratory illnesses began.

Over the next three months, Becky's columns of medical expenses lengthened. Bill looked at her journal and groaned. But I knew he was pleased Becky seemed to care.

Does she really? I wondered. Now and then, I began thinking so—until summer arrived, along with the chance to sleep late. But Becky had to care for Buttercup. "Why does she have to be fed at six o'clock, Mama?" she pleaded. "What's wrong with eight? It's vacation!"

There was no question at all about Buttercup's feelings toward Becky. While Bill and Scott struggled to halter-break young bulls and heifers, Buttercup now happily followed Becky around the ranch.

Fall and winter slid into spring. At 13 months, Buttercup weighed close to 500 pounds. She had huge brown eyes, four white socks and a coat that shined like mahogany. Although tiny horns now jutted above her ragged ears, she didn't show any of her mother's unwanted traits.

Becky was determined to win the blue ribbon at the county fair in September. "A show calf has to be perfect," Bill warned. But he hung the ID tag on the worst of Buttercup's ears, hoping to disguise the damage.

Becky began brushing the ears. "Hair will cover the notches," she said. "She'll be *almost* perfect."

July brought deadly heat, a profusion of flies and "pinkeye"—a blinding scourge of cattle. One morning, six weeks before the fair, Becky found Buttercup's face stained with muddy tears. A closer look revealed the swollen lids and white, unseeing eyes of the disease. Even with antibiotic therapy, recovery could take up to two months. "Daddy," Becky pleaded, "can you make her well in time?"

"We'll have to try." Together, Bill and Becky prepared the medicine, and Bill glued black patches over the heifer's eyes to protect them from glare, flies and dirt.

A week before the show, the patches were removed. We held our breath as Becky crouched in front of Buttercup. "All the brown's come back in her eyes," she cried. "She can see!"

Flags, mariachis, shouting children and bawling cattle added to the excitement at the Cochise County Fair. Judging day for cattle was Saturday. Buttercup was groomed and ready. So was Becky. At 3 p.m. she and the other contestants were waiting in line to show their heifers. Horns were polished, hoofs shellacked. Tails were teased and sprayed.

"She looks great, honey," Bill said. "Now, don't forget—buyers are in the crowd. If she wins, you'll get an offer, and she'll be gone"—he snapped his fingers—"just like that." Bill was surprised Becky didn't show more excitement. Wasn't this the big moment she'd been working for?

The gate opened, and Buttercup's competition entered the ring: five magnificent, big-boned, long-legged heifers. "They make Buttercup look so small," I whispered to Bill.

The judge, a rangy Texan, began checking each heifer carefully, then questioned its young owner. Most children talked about feeding schedules and weight gain. Becky's turn came last. "Tell me about your heifer, young lady," he said.

"Her name is Buttercup," Becky began, "and she's got the best pedigree in Arizona. She's by our KC Battle Prince 74 bull who was by W Battle Prince 10-12960305, who was by Domino Prince M194-11116795 ..."

The judge tipped his Stetson to the back of his head and smiled.

For three minutes, Becky recited the names and dozens of numbers she had so eagerly memorized. When she finished, the judge reached for the microphone. "Six fine heifers, ladies and gentlemen. But my choice for first place is this one." He pointed to Buttercup. "She'll be a strong addition to anyone's herd." Becky had won her blue ribbon.

By the time Bill and I pushed our way through the crowd, a buyer was already running his hand over Buttercup's hips. "Your dad around, miss?"

"Right here," Bill said. "Glad you like the heifer, but my daughter's the one who can tell you about her."

As Becky looked at the buyer, tears welled. "She was the best calf we ever had," she began. "But her knees swell up." Her lips trembled now. "She was frozen when she was born so she gets sick easily, and she needs somebody to love her all the time."

"Well, now," the buyer said, winking at Bill and me. "How 'bout I look at some of your other heifers?"

Reality has but one shape; hope is many shaped.

WOLFGANG VON GOETHE

Bill broke into a knowing smile. "Fine."

On the way home, Bill said, "Becky, let's turn Buttercup out to pasture. With the bloodlines she's got, she'll have one heck of a calf, don't you think?" Becky nodded and hugged her dad.

Four years later, Becky was ready for college. Before she left, we crossed the field to admire Buttercup's third calf. "Best calf of the year," Bill said.

Becky grinned. "Daddy, you always did say, 'It's all in the genes.' "

I looked at my husband and then at our daughter. She was still the math whiz, but now she was also a lover of animals and nature. *It is in the genes,* I thought. *They are so alike.*

"Hi, Butter," Becky murmured, as we reached the herd. The cow, with her calf at her side, ambled up and lowered her head to be scratched. "She never forgets me, does she?"

I smiled. I knew Becky would never forget her either—and someday she'd understand that Buttercup had helped her see what's truly important in life.

Through Buttercup, my daughter had learned about the feelings that make us who we are, even if they don't always add up like a nice column of numbers. For Becky, there was now a math of the heart—the math that matters most.

THE TERRIBLY, TRAGICALLY SAD MAN

BY

LOREN SEIBOLD

Once there was a boy who lived in a big house on a hill. He loved dogs and horses, sports cars and music. He climbed trees and went swimming, played football and admired pretty girls. Except for having to pick up after himself, he had a nice life.

One day the boy said to God, "I've been thinking, and I know what I want when I become a man."

"What?" asked God.

"I want to live in a big house with a porch across the front and two Saint Bernards and a garden out back. I want to marry a woman who is tall and very beautiful and kind, who has long, black hair and blue eyes, and who plays the guitar and sings in a clear, high voice.

"I want three strong sons to play football with. When they grow up, one will be a great scientist, one will be a Senator and the youngest will quarterback for the 49ers.

"I want to be an adventurer who sails vast oceans and climbs tall mountains and rescues people. And I want to drive a red Ferrari and never have to pick up after myself."

"That sounds like a nice dream," said God. "I want you to be happy."

One day, playing football, the boy hurt his knee. After that he couldn't climb tall mountains or even tall trees, much less sail vast oceans. So he studied marketing and started a medical-supplies business.

He married a girl who was very beautiful and very kind and who had long, black hair. But she was short, not tall, and had brown eyes, not blue. She couldn't play the guitar, or even sing. But she prepared wonderful meals seasoned with rare Chinese spices and painted magnificent pictures of birds.

Because of his business, he lived in a city near the top of a tall apartment building that overlooked the blue ocean and the city's twinkling lights. He didn't have room for two Saint Bernards, but he had a fluffy cat.

He had three daughters, all very beautiful. The youngest, who was in a wheelchair, was the loveliest. The three daughters loved their father very much. They didn't play football with him, but sometimes they went to the park and tossed a Frisbee — except for the youngest, who sat under a tree strumming her guitar and singing lovely, haunting songs.

He made enough money to live comfortably, but he didn't drive a red Ferrari. Sometimes he had to pick up things and put them away — even things that didn't belong to him. After all, he had three daughters.

Then one morning the man awoke and remembered his dream. "I am very sad," he said to his best friend.

"Why?" asked his friend.

"Because I once dreamed of marrying a tall woman with black hair and blue eyes who would play the guitar and sing. My wife can't play the guitar or sing. She has brown eyes, and she's not tall."

"Your wife is beautiful and very kind," said his friend. "She creates splendid pictures and delectable food."

But the man wasn't listening.

"I am very sad," the man confessed to his wife one day.

"Why?" asked his wife.

"Because I once dreamed of living in a big house with a porch, and of having two Saint Bernards and a garden out back. Instead, I live in an apartment on the 47th floor."

"Our apartment is comfortable, and we can see the ocean from our couch," replied his wife. "We have love, laughter and paintings of birds and a fluffy cat — not to mention three beautiful children."

But the man wasn't listening.

"I am very sad," the man said to his therapist.

"Why?" asked the therapist.

"Because I once dreamed that I would grow up to be a great adventurer. Instead, I'm a bald businessman with a bad knee."

"The medical supplies you sell have saved many lives," said the therapist.

But the man wasn't listening. So his therapist charged him $110 and sent him home.

"I am very sad," the man said to his accountant.

"Why?" asked the accountant.

"Because I once dreamed of driving a red Ferrari and of never having to pick up after myself. Instead, I take public transportation, and sometimes I still have to clean up."

"You wear good suits. You eat at fine restaurants, and you've toured Europe," said his accountant.

But the man wasn't listening. His accountant charged him $100 anyway. He was dreaming of a red Ferrari himself.

"I am very sad," the man said to his minister.

"Why?" asked the minister.

"Because I once dreamed of having three sons: a great scientist, a politician and a quarterback. Instead, I have three daughters, and the youngest can't even walk."

"But your daughters are beautiful and intelligent," said the minister. "They love you very much, and they've all done well. One is a nurse, another is an artist and the youngest teaches music to children."

But the man wasn't listening. He was so sad that he became very sick. He lay in a white hospital room surrounded by nurses in white uniforms. Tubes and wires connected his body to blinking machines that he had once sold to the hospital.

He was terribly, tragically sad. His family, friends and minister gathered around his bed. They were all deeply sad too. Only his therapist and his accountant remained happy.

Then one night, when everyone except the nurses had gone home, the man said to God, "Remember when I was a boy and I told you all the things I wanted?"

"It was a lovely dream," said God.

"Why didn't you give me those things?" asked the man.

"I could have," said God. "But I wanted to surprise you with things you didn't dream of.

"I suppose you've noticed what I've given you: a kind, beautiful wife; a good business; a nice place to live; three lovely daughters — one of the best packages I've put together — "

"Yes," interrupted the man. "But I thought you were going to give me what I really wanted."

"And I thought you were going to give me what I really wanted," said God.

"What did you want?" asked the man. It had never occurred to him that God was in want of anything.

No pessimist ever discovered the secrets of the stars or sailed to an uncharted land or opened a new heaven to the human spirit.

HELEN KELLER

"I wanted to make you happy with what I'd given you," said God.

The man lay in the dark all night, thinking. Finally he decided to dream a new dream, one he wished he'd dreamed years before. He decided to dream that what he wanted most were the very things he already had.

And the man got well and lived happily on the 47th floor, enjoying his children's beautiful voices, his wife's deep brown eyes and her glorious paintings of birds. And at night he gazed at the ocean and contentedly watched the lights of the city twinkling on, one by one.

Hope is a strange invention—

A Patent of the Heart—

In unremitting action

Yet never wearing out—

EMILY DICKINSON

CHARLIE TWO-SHOES AND THE AMERICAN DREAM

BY

DAVID PERLMUTT

On a landing strip outside Tsingtao, China, the U.S. Marine and the Chinese boy hugged. "Bullard," the child shouted over the drone of the transport planes, "you send for me? You bring me stateside, won't you?"

"Oh, yes, Charlie, someday we'll come back for you," Pfc. William Bullard told his young friend.

With those words, as a bitter wind howled on that February day in 1948, the Marine was gone. So were others who had treated this youngster like a brother—and made him one of them. As the plane roared from the runway, Bullard tearfully looked back through a window. The small boy was standing at attention, saluting. He was also crying.

His name was Tsui Chi Hsii, but the Marines called him Charlie Two-Shoes, because that's what it sounded like when he first told them his name. The Marines had come to the northern Chinese city of Tsingtao two months after World War II ended to disarm and repatriate remnants of the surrendered Japanese army.

140

Skirting the city were dozens of mud-hut villages with no electricity or running water. The villagers had only a few hens and the vegetables they grew. The people went for months without meat. For years and years they had known nothing but war and its horrors.

When the Americans arrived, Tsui Chi Hsii was small and frail, but the ten-year-old had a smile that lit up the dreary winter landscape and caught the attention of the soldiers in Love Company. He swapped his family's eggs and roasted peanuts for K-rations of Spam, tuna fish and beans. He also kept the company's campfires stoked.

With his parents' permission, Charlie came to live in the barracks. When the company commander found out, he bent the rules and let the boy stay. The Marines had a tailor make uniforms for him—greens for winter, khakis for summer, complete with a private's stripe on the sleeves.

He kept his bunk straight, his uniform pressed and his shoes spit-shined. Charlie paraded with his new friends and endured inspection. He even got a Marine haircut.

He picked up their slang. In the mess hall, he'd say, "This is great chow." It must have been, because weeks of military food, along with daily exercise, put muscles on his small body.

The Marines sent Charlie to a school for Americans, where he was taught by Catholic nuns. In a year, he could speak English well and was singing tunes by his favorites, Roy Rogers and Gene Autry. And under the nuns' guidance, he was becoming a devout Catholic.

Occasionally, Charlie visited home. Once when he had gone with friends to the local swimming hole, he returned to the Marine base with his uniform full of mud. A prejudiced guard at the gate called the corporal on duty and said, "We've got a little gook here who says he's in your company." In the background, the corporal could hear, "I no gook. I U.S. Marine."

Marines left and other Marines arrived, but the replacements always adopted Charlie Two-Shoes. Finally, the last Marine shipped out.

China's civil war was nearing its end, and Mao Zedong's troops moved into Tsingtao. The Bamboo Curtain dropped.

When Charlie returned to his home, his parents didn't know what to do. Aware that the Communists were the enemy of the Americans, they feared for their son's life. After four years with the Marines, he could barely speak his native language. Charlie's mother told his father to dig a hole big enough for the boy to hide in.

One day, Mao's soldiers found Charlie, who was still wearing his Marine greens. The soldiers said the Marines were now the enemy—he wasn't to think about them again. Charlie bit his tongue, but remained silent. When the men left, Charlie's mother began burning his Marine possessions—uniforms, books and papers, evidence that could be used against him. She asked for his green pants, but Charlie wouldn't let her destroy them. She dyed the trousers black.

The Communists left Charlie alone for a while. He went to high school, and on Sundays he'd walk 15 miles to St. Michael Cathedral in Tsingtao, until Mao shut the church and outlawed religion. Charlie continued to pray: "I have no place to worship, but I know you are with me." He felt sure that if being a Marine meant he had to sacrifice his life, he would go to heaven.

After high school, he went to an agriculture college, and the government hired him as a researcher in silk production. In the winter of 1960, Charlie married Zhu Jin Mie.

In 1962 his supervisor called him in. "It's been brought to my attention that you have a history with the American Marines," he told Charlie. "The party would appreciate it if you would provide us with information to convince our people that the Marines treated our people badly."

Charlie knew he could be executed for not cooperating, but he would not betray his Marine comrades. He said he'd forgotten the past.

A week later he was fired from his job and arrested. A court convicted him of suspicion of espionage and sentenced him to seven years in a labor camp and ten years under house arrest. Jin Mie was fired from her teaching position for refusing to divorce her husband, and was sent to work in the fields.

Charlie served his term and returned home. His son Jeff, two months old when his father left, was now seven. Charlie and Jin Mie soon had another son and a daughter. But, still under house arrest, Charlie was able to find only the most menial jobs. He dug wells and carried manure to the government vegetable fields.

Conditions eased after Richard Nixon's historic 1972 trip to China, and by 1979 Charlie's house arrest ended. Still, because of his record, Charlie continued to have trouble finding work. That's when someone suggested he contact his Marine friends. Perhaps he could find a job in the United States.

He asked the authorities for permission to write to America. They refused, but Charlie pestered them until they relented. Then he needed a miracle. His address books had been burned years before, and he couldn't recall his friends' addresses. "Lord, thank you for keeping me alive," he prayed. "You've got to help one more time. Help me remember my buddies' addresses."

Suddenly he was writing to three U.S. addresses he'd memorized 32 years earlier. One letter went to William Bullard in Autryville, N.C.

On his way home from an errand, Bill Bullard, 66, now a retired insurance salesman, reached into his mailbox. Buried in a stack of mail was a letter from China.

Hope arouses, as nothing else can arouse, a passion for the possible.

WILLIAM SLOANE COFFIN

143

"Dear Bullard—How are you and your family? Do you remember old buddy in China? Did you ever think of little Charlie? Yes, here I am writing to you. I hope you would be willing to give me help as you did before to create success."

Bullard couldn't believe his eyes. He rushed to a phone to call another Marine, Roy Sibit in Tallmadge, Ohio. "Sibit," Bullard said. "Charlie's alive!"

May 10, 1983, Cleveland Hopkins International Airport. Bullard, Sibit and three other former Marine buddies cried as the tiny man came off the jet. In all the years they hadn't heard from him, they'd still talked about him—and wondered if he was alive. When they were finally face to face, Charlie Tsui greeted the men with "Semper Fi," short for the Marine slogan *Semper Fidelis*—"always faithful."

By now Charlie's friends had written hundreds of letters to U.S. officials and the Chinese embassy, pressing for a six-month visitor's visa. It had taken three years, but finally he'd been allowed to come, and his buddies arranged to send him a ticket.

Tsui stayed with Sibit in Ohio. When his visa time ran out, he received an extension. But as that was ending, deportation loomed. Then Attorney General Edwin Meese stepped in. Charlie could stay indefinitely and also was allowed to send for his family. The 30 or so former Marines from Love Company helped raise $5000 to get the Tsuis settled in Greensboro, N.C.

Soon Charlie Tsui was helping manage a Chinese restaurant. Eighteen months later, he opened his own in Chapel Hill, named Tsing Tao after his hometown. Photos of a young Charlie with his Marines cover a back wall. Among his prized possessions are the black-dyed Marine trousers. They still fit.

Hope is the best possession. None are completely wretched but those who are without hope.

WILLIAM HAZLITT

"Sometimes I have to pinch myself to see if this is all real," Tsui says. "I have finally reached the American dream."

"A lot of people ask why we're so dedicated to Charlie and why we've stuck with him all these years," says Don Sexton, a former corporal with Love Company. "He was persecuted because of his relationship with us Marines. We consider him a brother. And you just don't desert a Marine brother."

A MIRACLE OF MERMAIDS

BY

MARGO PFEIFF

Rhonda Gill froze as she heard her four-year-old daughter, Desiree, sobbing quietly in the family room that morning in October 1993. Rhonda tiptoed through the doorway. The tiny dark-haired child was hugging a photograph of her father, who had died nine months earlier. Rhonda, 24, watched as Desiree gently ran her fingers around her father's face. "Daddy," she said softly, "why won't you come back?"

The petite brunette college student felt a surge of despair. It had been hard enough coping with her husband Ken's death, but her daughter's grief was more than she could bear. *If only I could tear the pain out of her,* Rhonda thought.

Ken Gill and Rhonda Hill of Yuba City, Calif., had met when Rhonda was 18, and had married after a whirlwind courtship. Their daughter, Desiree, was born on January 9, 1989.

Although a muscular six feet, three inches tall, Ken was a gentle man whom everyone loved. His big passion was his daughter. "She's a real daddy's girl," Rhonda would often say as Ken's eyes twinkled with pride.

Father and daughter went everywhere together: hiking, dune-buggy riding and fishing for bass and salmon on the Feather River.

Instead of gradually adjusting to her father's death, Desiree had refused to accept it. "Daddy will be home soon," she would tell her mother. "He's at work." When she played with her toy telephone, she pretended she was chatting with him. "I miss you, Daddy," she'd say. "When will you come back?"

Immediately after Ken's death, Rhonda moved from her apartment in Yuba City to her mother's home in nearby Live Oak. Seven weeks after the funeral, Desiree was still inconsolable. "I just don't know what to do," Rhonda told her mother, Trish Moore, a 47-year-old medical assistant.

One evening the three of them sat outside, gazing at the stars over the Sacramento Valley. "See that one, Desiree?" Her grandmother pointed at a bright speck near the horizon. "That's your daddy shining down from heaven." Several nights later Rhonda woke to find Desiree on the doorstep in her pajamas, weeping as she sought her daddy's star. Twice they took her to a child therapist, but nothing seemed to help.

As a last resort, Trish took Desiree to Ken's grave, hoping that it would help her come to terms with his death. The child laid her head against his gravestone and said, "Maybe if I listen hard enough I can hear Daddy talk to me."

Then one evening, as Rhonda tucked her child in, Desiree announced, "I want to die, Mommy, so I can be with Daddy." *God help me*, Rhonda prayed. *What more can I possibly do?*

November 8, 1993, would have been Ken's 29th birthday. "How will I send him a card?" Desiree asked her grandmother.

"How about if we tie a letter to a balloon," Trish said, "and send it up to heaven?" Desiree's eyes immediately lit up.

On their way to the cemetery, the back seat of the car full of flowers for their planned gravesite visit, the three stopped at a store. "Help

Mom pick out a balloon," Trish instructed. At a rack where dozens of helium-filled silver Mylar balloons bobbed, Desiree made an instant decision: "That one!" Happy Birthday was emblazoned above a drawing of the Little Mermaid from the Disney film. Desiree and her father had often watched the video together.

The child's eyes shone as they arranged flowers on Ken's grave. It was a beautiful day, with a slight breeze rippling the eucalyptus trees. Then Desiree dictated a letter to her dad. "Tell him 'Happy Birthday. I love you and miss you,' " she rattled off. " 'I hope you get this and can write me on my birthday in January.' "

Trish wrote the message and their address on a small piece of paper, which was then wrapped in plastic and tied to the end of the string on the balloon. Finally Desiree released the balloon.

For almost an hour they watched the shining spot of silver grow ever smaller. "Okay," Trish said at last. "Time to go home." Rhonda and Trish were beginning to walk slowly from the grave when they heard Desiree shout excitedly, "Did you see that? I saw Daddy reach down and take it!" The balloon, visible just moments earlier, had disappeared. "Now Dad's going to write me back," Desiree declared as she walked past them toward the car.

On a cold, rainy November morning on Prince Edward Island in eastern Canada, 32-year-old Wade MacKinnon pulled on his waterproof duck-hunting gear. MacKinnon, a forest ranger, lived with his wife and three children in Mermaid, a rural community a few miles east of Charlottetown.

But instead of driving to the estuary where he usually hunted, he suddenly decided to go to Mermaid Lake, two miles away. Leaving his pickup, he hiked past dripping spruce and pine and soon entered a cranberry bog surrounding the 23-acre lake. In the bushes on the shoreline, something fluttered and caught his eye. Curious, he approached to find a silver balloon snagged in the branches of a thigh-high bayberry bush. Printed on one side was a picture of a mermaid. When he untangled the string, he found a soggy piece of paper at the end of it, wrapped in plastic.

At home, MacKinnon carefully removed the wet note, allowing it to dry. When his wife, Donna, came home later, he said, "Look at this," and showed her the balloon and note. Intrigued, she read: "November 8, 1993. Happy Birthday, Daddy ..." It finished with a mailing address in Live Oak, Calif.

"It's only November 12," Wade exclaimed. "This balloon traveled 3000 miles in four days!"

"And look," said Donna, turning the balloon over. "This is a Little Mermaid balloon, and it land-ed at Mermaid Lake."

"We have to write to Desiree," Wade said. "Maybe we were chosen to help this little girl." But he could see that his wife didn't feel the same way. With tears in her eyes, Donna stepped away from the balloon. "Such a young girl having to deal with death—it's awful," she said.

Wade let the matter rest. He placed the note in a drawer and tied the balloon, still buoyant, to the railing of the balcony overlooking their living room. But the sight of the balloon made Donna uncom-fortable. A few days later, she stuffed it in a closet.

As the weeks went by, however, Donna found herself thinking more and more about the balloon. It had flown over the Rocky Mountains and the Great Lakes. Just a few more miles and it would have landed in the ocean. Instead it had stopped there, in Mermaid.

Our three children are so lucky, she thought. *They have two healthy parents.* She imagined how their daughter, Hailey, almost two years old, would feel if Wade were to die.

The next morning, Donna said to Wade: "You're right. We have this balloon for a reason. We have to try to help Desiree."

In a Charlottetown bookstore Donna MacKinnon bought an adaptation of *The Little Mermaid*. A few days later, just after Christmas, Wade brought home a birthday card that read "For a Dear Daughter, Loving Birthday Wishes."

Donna sat down one morning to write a letter to Desiree. When she finished, she tucked it into the birthday card, wrapped it up with the book and mailed the package on January 3, 1994.

Desiree's fifth birthday came and went quietly with a small party on January 9. Every day since they'd released the balloon, Desiree had asked Rhonda, "Do you think Daddy has my balloon yet?" After her party she stopped asking.

Late on the afternoon of January 19, the MacKinnons' package arrived. Busy cooking dinner, Trish looked at the unfamiliar return address and assumed it was a birthday gift for her granddaughter from someone in Ken's family. Rhonda and Desiree had moved back to Yuba City, so Trish decided to deliver it to Rhonda the next day.

As Trish watched television that evening, a thought nagged at her. Why would someone send a parcel for Desiree to this address? Tearing the package open, she found the card. "For a Dear Daughter…" Her heart raced. *Dear God!* she thought, and reached for the telephone. It was after midnight, but she had to call Rhonda.

When Trish, eyes red from weeping, pulled into Rhonda's driveway the next morning at 6:45, her daughter and granddaughter were already up.

Hope deferred makes the heart sick, but a desire fulfilled is a tree of life.

PROVERBS 13

Rhonda and Trish sat Desiree between them on the couch. Trish said, "Desiree, this is for you," and handed her the parcel. "It's from your daddy."

"I know," said Desiree matter-of-factly. "Here, Grandma, read it to me."

"Happy birthday from your daddy," Trish began. "I guess you must be wondering who we are. Well, it all started in November when my husband, Wade, went duck hunting. Guess what he found? A mermaid balloon that you sent your daddy…" Trish paused. A single tear began to trickle down Desiree's cheek. "There are no stores in heaven, so your daddy wanted someone to do his shopping for him. I think he picked us because we live in a town called Mermaid."

Trish continued reading: "I know your daddy would want you to be happy and not sad. I know he loves you very much and will always be watching over you. Lots of love, the MacKinnons."

When Trish finished reading, she looked at Desiree. "I knew Daddy would find a way not to forget me," the child said.

Wiping the tears from her eyes, Trish put her arm around Desiree and began to read *The Little Mermaid* that the MacKinnons had sent. The story was different from the one Ken had so often read to the child. In that version, the Little Mermaid lives happily ever after with the handsome prince. But in the new one, she dies because a wicked witch has taken her tail. Three angels carry her away.

As Trish finished reading, she worried that the ending would upset her granddaughter. But Desiree put her hands on her cheeks with delight. "She goes to heaven!" she cried. "That's why Daddy sent me this book. Because the mermaid goes to heaven just like him!"

In mid-February the MacKinnons received a letter from Rhonda: "On January 19 my little girl's dream came true when your parcel arrived."

During the next few weeks, the MacKinnons and the Gills often telephoned each other. Then, in March, Rhonda, Trish and Desiree flew to Prince Edward Island to meet the MacKinnons. As the two families walked through the forest on snowshoes to see the spot beside the lake where Wade had found the balloon, Rhonda and Desiree fell silent. It seemed as though Ken was there with them.

"People tell me, 'What a coincidence that your mermaid balloon landed so far away at a place called Mermaid Lake,'" says Rhonda. "But we know Ken picked the MacKinnons as a way to send his love to Desiree. She understands now that her father is with her always."

Many waters cannot quench love,

neither can floods drown it.

SONG OF SOLOMAN 8

HERO OF THE 'HOOD

BY

PAULA MCDONALD

Around midnight, 15-year-old Mike Powell took a deep breath and pushed himself reluctantly from the dilapidated chair. Although he had done this many times before, it never got easier.

He stood quietly, looking down at the six sleeping children. Gently he shook eight-year-old Amber. "Time to go," he whispered. The oldest of his five sisters moaned.

Mike moved to the foot of the bed and leaned over his brother. "It's time, Raffie," he said. The 11-year-old burrowed deeper under the single blanket the children shared. Six-year-old Chloe began to cry, "I don't want to go. It's dark!"

"We got to go," Mike replied. "Mom owes somebody money."

The little girl knew the routine and staggered sleepily to her small pile of clothes on the floor. As four-year-old Shanice sat up in bed, Amber stuffed diapers into the stroller. Mike and Raf carefully dressed the sleeping babies, Ebony, two, and Michellé, three months.

With Mike leading the way, the stumbling little band moved silently down the back stairway of the hotel and onto the ominous inner-city streets. Mike had no idea where his mother was—or where he would go next. He knew only that he had to find shelter for his family and keep them safe, no matter what.

From the time he was nine, Mike had been the only real parent his younger siblings had known, doing whatever he could to protect them from South Central Los Angeles's "Jungle"—a combat zone of drug wars and gang slayings. He had braved brutalization at home and terror on the streets to keep his family together. But tonight he was running dry.

When Mike was born on December 29, 1977, in L.A., his father, Fonso Powell, was in prison for drug dealing. Mike's 15-year-old mother, Cheryl, dropped out of school to support the baby. "My life could have been different without you," she would later tell Mike.

When Mike was four, Fonso, a six-foot-five, 300-pound veteran, was released from prison. He found steady work as a carpenter and gave up drugs.

Although Fonso made Mike and Cheryl feel safer, he had severe psychological problems, and his discipline was harrowing. For minor infractions like slamming a door he would force Mike to do pushups for hours. If the boy collapsed, his father would beat him. So fanatical was Fonso's insistence on school attendance that Cheryl had to hide Mike in a closet when he was sick.

Perhaps it was some dark premonition that drove Fonso to toughen up his young son and teach him self-reliance. He taught Mike to cook and shop, and forced him to solve problems far beyond his years. "You gotta be a man," he would say. Fonso also warned Mike to stay away from drugs and crime: "If I ever catch you doing that, I'll kill you!"

Fonso, however, drifted back into the world of fast money. In 1986 he was murdered in a run-in with drug dealers. Overnight, the security and income Fonso had provided was gone. It was back to the streets for

155

24-year-old Cheryl and her soon-to-be-four children: Mike; Raf, four; Chloe, two; and another baby on the way.

Soon Cheryl brought home a man named Marcel, a cocaine addict who began terrorizing the family. "Milk is for me!" he would sneer as Mike tried to keep him from drinking his baby sister's milk. "From now on, kids here drink water!" When Mike questioned what Marcel had done with Cheryl's wages as a transit worker, Marcel broke the little boy's jaw.

Marcel got Cheryl hooked on cocaine, and the two would disappear on drug binges, leaving the children alone for weeks at a time.

Mike became adept at covering up for Cheryl with curious neighbors. "My mother's at work … at the doctor's … shopping" went the litany of excuses. Cheryl had convinced the youngster that if he let anyone know what was happening, the children would be sent to separate foster homes.

For Mike and his siblings, home was always a brief pit stop at best. Whenever he learned that Cheryl had disappeared with the rent money and the family was to be evicted, he would quietly move the children at night to avoid revealing their parentless status to authorities. Cheryl and Marcel always caught up with them.

One night Marcel became enraged with Mike and told Cheryl, "Get him out of here!" Mike was stunned when his mother hurried him to the door and pushed him out. It was 3 a.m., and he was wearing only a T-shirt, pajama bottoms and slippers. Fighting back tears, he walked three hours to his grandparents' apartment and invented a story about running away from home, blaming himself.

Cheryl's parents, Mabel and Otis Bradley, loved their grandchildren deeply. But they worked long hours and lived a difficult multiple-bus commute away, so they could see them only rarely. Sensing the family was struggling, Mabel sent toys, clothes and diapers. She never dreamed her gifts were being sold for drug money.

Mabel's constant phone calls and unconditional love became Mike's only anchor of support, but he still didn't reveal that anything was wrong. He feared his gentle grandmother would have a heart attack if she learned the truth.

To make sure no one suspected anything, Mike began cleaning the apartment himself, doing laundry by hand and keeping his sisters fed, diapered and spotless. He learned to scavenge junk shops, finding hairbrushes, bottles and diapers—whatever they could afford.

At nine, Mike quit school to support the family. He cleaned yards, unloaded trucks and stocked liquor stores, always working before dawn or late at night so the smaller children wouldn't be alone while awake. With the family's many moves, the school system never noticed he was gone.

Mike became an expert at enrolling his siblings in school when Cheryl was not available. He would plead with a stranger to call the new school for him and claim to be a working mother or father who was sending an older son to register the children. To classmates and teachers, the other children always looked normal and well-groomed. No one could have imagined how they were forced to live or that they were being raised by another child.

As Cheryl became more desperate for drugs, she had frequent brushes with the law. Over the next few years she was jailed for possession and sale of narcotics. Out of jail, Cheryl bore more children—Shanice in 1989 and Ebony in 1991.

More than ever, Mike insisted the older children attend school. "You don't have to end up on the street," he told them. "You can go to college." Their situation was his best motivational tool. "See what Mamma is like?" he would say. "Stay off drugs!"

Make melody to our God upon the lyre . . . hope in his steadfast love.

PSALM 147

157

Most important, Mike was always protecting his siblings. When Cheryl got high, Mike would take the frightened children into another room and play games to distract them. Somehow he managed to sort through the brutal methods of his father and blend them with the loving example of his grandmother to form a unique value system. In return, the children adored him.

With Cheryl gone for up to a year at a time, the family's finances grew desperate. Yet Mike refused to fall into the easy world of drugs.

What the youngster did do was go out late at night to sell doctored macadamia nuts in other neighborhoods. To half-crazed addicts, the nuts looked like $30 crack-cocaine "rocks." But two or three quick sales in any one place were all Mike could make before the addicts caught on. If Mike was around when they came looking for him, he would be killed. By age 15, he'd been shot more than half a dozen times, most often as a bystander caught in gang or drug wars.

With the birth of Michellé in 1993, there were now six siblings to support, and the situation became critical. One Christmas there was only a can of corn, some Spam and a box of macaroni and cheese for all of them to share. Their only toys for the past year had been one McDonald's Happy Meal figurine for each child. For presents, Mike had the children wrap the figurines in newspaper and exchange them. It was one of their better Christmases.

Mike's desperation grew by the day. For as long as he could remember, he had lived with relentless daily fears: *Will the rent get paid? Will we eat? Will we be on the street tonight?*

It was then—on that desperate night in the hotel—that Mike woke his siblings and hustled them away. This time, after more than 40 moves, "home" became the Frontier Hotel, a terrifying dive in L.A.'s skid row where pimps and prostitutes stalked the neighborhood.

One morning at about two o'clock, Mike struggled out of a troubled sleep. His brother and sisters were huddled under one blanket on the floor. Michellé was crying, but there was no food for her. The boy who had shouldered his burden for so many years suddenly lost hope.

Stumbling over to a window in despair, he stood at the edge, steeling himself to jump. Silently asking his siblings to forgive him, he closed his eyes and took a last deep breath.

Just then, a woman across the street spotted him and began screaming. Mike reeled back from the edge. As her screams continued, he ducked back into the room and fell into a corner, sobbing. All night, he rocked the hungry baby and prayed for help.

It came on the day before Thanksgiving 1993. Cheryl had returned and was walking with Mike along the street when they passed a group offering free food for the needy. They were volunteers for the Hiding Place, a nondenominational church. Cheryl belligerently asked for a dozen extra sandwiches for the "six other kids" at home. The volunteers, conned so often, rolled their eyes. But Mike vouched for his mother, and one volunteer, 22-year-old Bjorn Park, handed Cheryl the extra sandwiches.

Mike later brought the kids back to the church workers to prove he wasn't lying. So impressed were they with him and his polite siblings that they began asking gentle questions. A dam deep inside Mike finally broke, and his story spilled out.

The next day Park went to the Frontier Hotel to drive the children to the Santa Monica Civic Auditorium, where church groups were providing Thanksgiving dinners. Stunned by conditions in the hotel, he invited the kids to live at his home until other safe shelter could be found.

The church group tried to find the family a permanent residence, but no private home could take on all the children. Mike insisted that his family be kept together. What's more, only one person he knew loved the children as much as he did: his grandmother. He was adamant that she and his grandfather become their guardians—despite their age and income—as long as the Bradleys agreed.

When Mike finally told his grandparents the truth, Mabel and Otis were horrified. "I won't have them in foster homes," Mabel said. "We're all they have." In 1996, Mabel and Otis became the children's legal guardians.

Formerly retired, Mabel returned to work as a clerk-typist; Otis cares for Michellé and Ebony while the older children attend school. Through the contributions of Mabel's co-workers, the Bradleys were able to buy a small house in Fontana, 50 miles east of L.A. Although it means a daily commute of over 100 miles for Mabel, she is thrilled. "The children have a yard to play in," she says. For their part, Amber, Chloe and Raf are known in school for being hard workers, and have earned many awards.

In February 1994, through the Hiding Place, 16-year-old Mike met former drug addict Mike Huante, Jr., 22, and construction worker Ray Diggs, 26. Huante and Diggs got Mike a job as a pipe fitter, and invited him to join their inspirational rap group, Positively Hardcore, in their mission to carry a message of hope to inner-city kids.

Two years later Tapestry Records, a new label, agreed to finance their first music video. And, simultaneously, a strange coincidence gave them an even bigger chance at a future career. One of the songs in the movie *Normal Life* was being pulled at the last minute. Lisa Marie Barry, who did marketing for the film's distributor and who was a volunteer at the Hiding Place, had heard the group's song, "Ril Criminals," and recommended it. The film's director put the song on the soundtrack, and *Normal Life* was released in October 1996.

While Mike is dedicated to reaching out to inner-city youngsters, he is most gratified by the knowledge that his siblings are thriving. Recently, Mike stood in front of his grandparents' home and knocked on the door. Immediately, he was bowled over by a rush of children, squealing and clinging to his legs. As Mike gathered all of them in, he thought with relief, *They're safe now, and they're still together.* Mike felt his life had turned out to be a lucky miracle after all.

While it takes courage to achieve greatness, it takes more courage to find fulfillment in being ordinary. What is the adventure in being ordinary? It is daring to love just for the pleasure of giving it away. It is venturing to give new life and to nurture it to maturity. It is working hard for the pure joy of being tired at the end of the day. It is caring and sharing and giving and loving, because we trust our ordinary lives in the hands of an extraordinary God. There are no Oscars or medals awarded for any of these pursuits. But then, no piece of gold or bronze statuette can sum up their worth.

MARILYN THOMSEN

"HE HAS NOT LEFT ME"

BY
JOYCE BROTHERS

*M*y husband was tall, trim and handsome. He played squash three times a week and rode his bike for miles. Weekends he gardened, cut brush, sanded floors, put up shelves. Milt was a supremely healthy man.

Then in his early 50s, he developed hypertension. His internist put him on medication and advised him to stop smoking. A few years later, he developed a heart flutter. His doctor prescribed more medication and again asked him to stop smoking.

Milt was a physician. He knew that tobacco causes cancer and death. Yet he smoked like a furnace. Now he told me he wasn't going to smoke anymore. But he didn't really stop — he just wouldn't smoke when I was around.

On the morning of July 2, 1987, two days before our 38th wedding anniversary, Milt noticed blood in his urine. On July 9, he checked into New York's Mount Sinai Hospital, where he had been on staff almost all our married life. The surgeon found a malignant polyp inside his bladder. He cut it out and told us he thought he had gotten it all. Milt would need a checkup every three months, but the prognosis was good.

Though Milt was optimistic, I remained worried. I learned that bladder cancer kills some 9700 Americans a year, and half these cases are caused by smoking.

By late summer Milt resumed his practice. At times his clothes smelled of smoke when he came home at night. I think he tried, but even knowing he was putting his life at risk, he found it impossible to stop. Still, he was feeling stronger, and we picked up the threads of our life. It was a time of closeness for us, happier still because of our narrow escape from disaster.

In October, Milt went into the hospital for his first checkup. "Everything appears fine," his surgeon told us. "But we won't know for sure until we get the biopsy results on Monday."

Monday dragged on and on. It was after 5 p.m. when the call came. Milt listened intently. At one point, a tear trickled down his cheek. I had never seen him cry before.

Finally, he said, "Well, thank you," and hung up. The cancer had reappeared. I threw my arms around him. "You're strong," I told him. "You can beat it."

He ran his finger around my face and summoned a half smile. "I'll do my damnedest," he promised. "I've got a lot to live for."

I'd had a dream that death was in bed with me. Death was a man, a strong, burly man. Curled up facing away from him, I could feel the hair on his chest, the stubble on his chin. I could smell his breath. I knew death had me in his grasp.

Milt underwent a risky but successful eight-hour operation to have his bladder removed. I learned that he would almost surely be impotent. But I assured him that life itself was all that mattered now.

Milt never smoked again after the surgery — it took a scare of this magnitude to make him stop. As soon as he quit, his heart flutter went away. I could not help thinking, *If you had only stopped 20 years ago, none of this would have happened.* How could he have been so stupid! I was angry. I am still angry about this.

Milt's recovery seemed to go well, and he began seeing patients again. But in January 1988 he got a pain in his abdomen, and another exam showed that the cancer had spread.

Milt's oncologist started him on chemotherapy. The side effects were horrendous: his hair began to fall out, he got exhausting hiccups and he was in constant pain. I was able to stop his hiccups with gentle massages. I would also brush his hair. He grumbled that I was babying him, but he loved it. I loved doing it. These were peaceful hours, and I felt overwhelmed by my love for him.

By spring, Milt had to close his office. He got hundreds of letters and calls, which cheered him immensely. I don't think he had realized quite how much his patients liked him and how very important he was to them.

Milt's had been a very special practice. He took medicine seriously, but he liked to have fun. He told terrible jokes, and every Friday afternoon he held a "medical conference." That's what he called it, but it was really a party for the nurses. A saleswoman who examined Milt's accounts before we sold the practice told me, "I have never seen a doctor who carried so many people on the books." After final negotiations I took one last look around. The lawyer said, "There's nothing special about this office, except that the walls are filled with laughter."

Milt was now in and out of the hospital so often that my visits to him there seem like a blur. In our conversations we never talked about

It is only the souls that do not love that go empty in this world.

ROBERT HUGH BENSON

166

death. Instead we would say, "When I get back on my feet . . ." or "As soon as you regain your strength . . . ." We always kept the future open.

For both of us, reminiscence, too, became a pleasure and comfort. "Remember when . . . ?" Milt would say, and we'd start talking about old times. We had a lifetime of memories. I held every one of them close.

He seemed to be feeling stronger one sunny October morning, so I drove him up to our farm in the country. We stopped to buy eggs from the woman down the road so we could have our ritual weekend breakfast. Milt made the coffee and eggs. Fried eggs were his culinary specialty. He had a frying pan dedicated to eggs. I was not allowed to use it for anything — he never even let me wash it. I made the toast and squeezed the orange juice. He ate everything. I was thrilled — he had not eaten that much for weeks.

After breakfast, he went upstairs alone and looked around. Each bedroom represented long weekends of hard work. Over the years we had scraped and painted until each room was fresh and welcoming.

Then he went outside. I watched him stand looking at the meadow where our daughter, Lisa, had been married 12 years before. I watched as he walked down to the brook where he and our grandson Micah used to fish.

He rested awhile, and then we got ready to leave. The last thing he said as he locked the door behind us was, "It's so beautiful here." There was a wistful note in his voice. We both knew he would probably never see the farm again.

That fall and winter, Milt's health went steadily downhill. The cancer spread to his bones.

He grew weaker, thinner — and angrier. I understood. After all, life is sweet; who wants it to end?

When Lisa's fourth child, a girl, was born January 6, 1989, I booked a flight to Iowa to see the baby. "Give her a kiss from me," Milt told me from his hospital bed.

The next day, I held little Ariel in my arms. I kissed her, and kissed her again for her grandfather. But I stayed only an hour. I felt uneasy being away from Milt.

Once home, I was tired and thought I'd wait to see Milt in the morning. Something made me change my mind. I went to the hospital and up to his room. When I took his hand, he opened his eyes.

"Oh, Joyce," he said. "Sit down."

He closed his eyes again, and I sat beside him, holding his hand. I talked for hours, telling him about Lisa's new baby and about our other grandchildren. I reminisced about our courtship, about the farm, about everything that had been important to me in our life together. Then I told him over and over how much I loved him and how happy he had always made me. I do not know if he heard me. Finally, well after midnight, the nurses told me I had to go. My telephone woke me before 6 a.m. Milt had just died.

When I walked into his hospital room, Milt was still lying in the bed. He looked peaceful; the cruel lines of pain had left his face. I kissed him good-by.

There was no time for grief. There were only details: people to notify, flowers to order, the funeral to arrange. I was too busy and numb to feel anything, which was a blessing.

At the service, two of Milt's colleagues spoke about him, and their sweet words pleased and comforted me. I was hungry to hear people talk about him. The hardest moment came at the cemetery. There is nothing worse than watching the coffin of a loved one being lowered into the raw ground.

Still, it was not until a few days later that I really grasped that Milt was gone. Then it hit me: he would never walk through the door. Never hold me again. I got up and made coffee and contemplated the rest of my life, with tears streaming down my face.

As a psychologist, I had lectured and written about grief and loneliness hundreds of times. But suddenly I was facing them myself, a new, unknown territory, and the pain was horrendous, unceasing and cruel. I'd cry when I reached out in the night and Milt was not there. I'd pass a restaurant he and I used to like, and tears would start anew.

The standard reaction to a widow's tears is to say, "There, there. You mustn't cry. Tears won't help." But tears *do* help. They are a kind of emotional first aid. A widow will stop when she no longer needs to cry. I went through months of obsessive remembering. And every memory triggered tears.

When someone asked me if I felt angry at Milt, I was shocked. Angry with my husband? Never!

But I was. Whenever I thought about his having smoked all those years, knowing full well that cigarettes can kill, I was enraged. There were so many things we had looked forward to doing together. Our life was truly golden. Now all of it had been snatched away by those lousy cigarettes.

It was nearly a year before I was able to think of Milt without crying. The turning point came when I remembered how he used to call me the Cabinet Lady. I tend to leave cabinet doors open when I'm cooking. Milt would say, "I see the Cabinet Lady is here. You're going to hurt yourself one of these days." And I'd reply, "I'm too short to hit my head."

One day I ran head-on into an open cabinet door and raised a huge bump on my forehead. After the "ouch!" I thought about Milt's millions of warnings. Despite the pain, I smiled.

But my greatest weapon for recovery was something Milt had told me after my father passed away. "He has not left you," Milt said. "Children always carry with them a part of their parents' souls. Husbands and wives remain part of each other."

I knew he was right. Milt *was* part of me. From that time on, life gradually began to brighten again. I still said "our" and "we," and I still cried, but less and less. It had been a hard year, a terrible year. I had felt that loneliness would eat me alive. But I had survived.

Today I am more accepting of the changes I've faced. I have started looking beyond my own horizon. My grief has also, I think, made me more sympathetic and sensitive to people. I have learned how comforting a few understanding words — and shared tears — can be.

I will always have a pocket of sorrow in my heart, but that will not keep me from plunging into life again. It will make me value every living minute, because I know how precious each one is. And I will speak out against smoking whenever I can.

The second spring after Milt died, I had another dream, and it was like a gift. We were at the farm, just the two of us. It was snowing, but the house was warm, with a fire blazing on the hearth.

Then, suddenly, Milt and I were outdoors in bright sunlight. We were holding hands and laughing, slipping on the snow as we made our way down the hill. But when we got to the brook, a miracle: daffodils were blooming on low, woody bushes. The trees blossomed with roses and daisies. And Milt was no longer bone-thin and drawn, no longer angry, no longer ravaged by cancer. We went back to the house together, our arms full of flowers.

If it were not for hopes, the heart would break.

THOMAS FULLER

THE PUNK AND THE TYRANT

BY

JOHN S. TOMPKINS

As a child, Nelson Diebel was hyperactive and always in trouble. His kindergarten teacher in Western Springs, Ill., demanded that he be dismissed, and in third grade doctors wanted to tranquilize him.

When Nelson was in seventh grade, his parents divorced, and his mischievous pranks turned to tantrums and fights at school. He began to drink and to smoke marijuana. Eventually, the boy was enrolled in The Peddie School in Hightstown, N.J., which saw potential in him. The boarding school required every student to participate in athletics and other extracurricular activities. On his application, Nelson wrote "swimming," even though he had never been serious about the sport. Soon, he was invited to meet Chris Martin, the swimming coach.

"He's a bright kid, but he needs attention," Peddie's admissions director told Martin. "If you're willing to work with him, we'll accept him."

Coach Martin, a handsome six-foot-three-inch, 230-pound task-master, knew of Nelson's troubled background from the application form. Yet he perceived a kind of fire inside the teen-ager, and suspected that if Nelson's anger could be channeled, there was no telling what he could achieve.

"The first thing I want you to know is that I am a tyrant," Martin told Nelson. He detailed the torturous routine Nelson could expect as a Peddie swimmer: 11/2 hour practices in the morning and 21/2 hours in the evening, gym workouts and weight training. Then he finished with a warning: "If you swim for me, you are going to do what I say, when I say, how I say."

Chris Martin had come to love swimming as a child in Harleysville, Pa., and he learned early the value of hard work. In swimming, he figured, you can't blame your failure on anyone else. And the more you practice, the better you perform. These lessons helped Martin earn acceptance to Yale, where he studied economics and was on the swim team.

When Martin began working at Peddie in 1986, he had already formulated a plan: he would mold high-school swimmers into world champions by driving them hard and constantly exposing them to his philosophy that you work until you can't work anymore—and then keep working. Only great effort leads to great rewards. "There is no doubt in my mind," he told friends, "that I'm going to have swimmers on the Olympic team someday."

Overpowered by the force of Martin's personality, Nelson agreed to the coach's terms, even though he wasn't really interested in swimming. He had already decided to report to practice for a couple of weeks and then quit. But when Nelson went to see the coach about dropping out of the program, Martin declared, "No chance! I'm going to make a swimmer out of you if I have to kill you."

One day at the pool, Nelson bragged that he could beat the school record of 58.5 seconds for the 100-yard breast stroke, despite having just been clocked at an embarrassing one minute, eight seconds. Everyone laughed—except Coach Martin. Over the weeks, Martin kept

Only great effort leads to great rewards

challenging Nelson, reminding him that nobody thought he could do it. "But anything is possible," he said, "if you really go after it."

For Nelson, the number 58.5 became an obsession. The truth was, Nelson Diebel secretly wanted to be a winner at something.

In two months, Nelson pared his time to 1:05. Then he hit a plateau at 1:04.6, and that held week after week no matter how hard he tried. Then one day when he felt he couldn't swim another stroke, he pared his time to 1:03 flat.

Some of his teammates still taunted him about his boast, but increasingly they accepted him. And he was surprised to find that he liked the sense of belonging.

By March 1987, Nelson was swimming 30 to 40 hours a week, and his time continued to improve. Coach Martin kept pushing, constantly putting new goals in front of him, always trying to turn his anger into a strength. "You'll never qualify for the Junior Nationals," he said, "because you're not willing to train like a champion." Nelson, as the coach expected, just gritted his teeth and the next day swam even faster. He eventually qualifed by cutting his time to 1:00.

At the Junior Nationals in April, Nelson hit 59 seconds in his preliminary heat, and later that evening he placed fifth in the finals, breaking The Peddie School record. For the first time in his life, he began to think he could be good at something. But his moment of triumph wasn't long-lasting. Coach Martin briefly praised his performance, then reminded him he could still do better.

At Peddie, students have a mandatory two-hour study period six nights a week. But Nelson couldn't sit still in one place that long, and nobody could make him.

One night Martin walked into Nelson's room, put a ten-dollar bill on the desk and said, "Sit here for 15 straight minutes, and you keep it." Then the coach placed a chair in front of the door and camped there, reading.

Seconds turned into minutes. Nelson fidgeted. He scratched his head. He pulled on an ear lobe. He looked at the clock on his desk. After what seemed an hour, only four minutes had passed. Nelson's eyes watered, and he pounded the desk with his fist. Coach Martin just sat. Nelson didn't win the ten dollars that evening, but the coach continued to check on him. Gradually, as the discipline of swimming matured him, Nelson was able to sit still and study for the two hours.

During the summer of 1987 Nelson won both the 100- and 200-meter breast stroke at the Junior Nationals. His times qualified him for the Olympic Trials a year later, where he placed eighth in the 200-meter and fifth in the 100-meter breaststroke events. Suddenly Nelson started thinking, *In another four years, I can make the Olympic team.*

Practically the only thing Nelson could think about now was the 1992 Olympics in Barcelona, Spain. He was so excited, it was harder than usual to sit still. This was especially true while on lifeguard duty at the Peddie pool, a boring job for a hyperactive teen-ager. During rest periods every hour, to break the monotony he would leap ten feet out from the railing of the spectators' balcony and 20 feet down into the deep end of the pool.

One afternoon, just three days after the 1988 Olympic Trials, Nelson leaned forward to jump—and slipped on the wet railing. Instinctively, he put out his hands, slammed onto the tile deck with both arms outstretched, then fell unconscious into the pool.

When he got word of the accident, Martin ran to the pool, praying that Nelson wasn't dead. Another student had seen Nelson fall and had pulled him from the water. Martin saw Nelson being placed on an ambulance stretcher, semiconscious and in shock. Later, at Princeton Medical Center, when the coach was shown X-rays of Nelson's hands, he feared that he would never again compete as a world-class swimmer.

Margaret Diebel flew in from Chicago that night. Her son's hands and wrists were too swollen for immediate surgery. They lay on the sheets, shattered—along with his Olympic hopes. A week later, in a two-hour operation, pins were inserted in his hands and forearms, and metal screws in his right wrist. The surgeon then manipulated the bones into place. When Nelson woke, both hands and forearms were in casts, and the doctor warned that he would probably never have more than 60-percent mobility in his hands and wrists. Visions of Barcelona '92 were fading as Nelson began to accept that he might never again swim in a meet.

Chris Martin drove Nelson and his mother from the hospital back to Peddie. When they arrived on campus, Martin parked the car and turned to the boy.

"You're either coming all the way back from this or we're going to stop doing business together. I don't want to hear halfway. I am going to torture you, and you are going to win national championships. If you're not committed to that, we're going to stop right now."

When the casts were taken off eight weeks later, Nelson's hands were so atrophied he could barely move them. Still, Martin ordered him into the pool. Nelson couldn't swim, but Martin insisted that he exercise his legs.

Nelson spent hour after painful hour flexing his wrists outside the pool and exercising his legs in the water. Late one afternoon he told the coach he was too tired to go on. Martin said nothing. He simply pulled all the ladders out of the pool, turned out the lights and left.

Hope is the dream of the waking man.

ARISTOTLE

The only way Nelson could get out of the water without using his fragile wrists was to hook his elbows through the rungs of a ladder—and now there were no ladders. In order to stay afloat, he had to keep kicking. Twenty minutes later, Martin returned and put the ladders back in the water. Later, Nelson learned that the coach had watched him from the darkened spectators' balcony. He'd proved again that Nelson could do more than he thought he could. A few weeks later, Nelson was swimming.

"The only thing holding you back is this," he told Nelson, pointing to his head. "If you believe in yourself, you can do anything."

Five months later, Nelson won the 200-yard breast stroke in the 1989 spring Nationals. When he graduated from Peddie in 1990, he enrolled at Princeton, and then decided to take his sophomore year off to train for the Olympics. At the trials on March 1, 1992, after months of almost nonstop training, Nelson set the U.S. record for the 100-meter breast stroke in the morning, then broke it later that same day in the finals.

But in the months leading up to the Olympics, others in the swimming world had doubts about his ability to win. He'd been ranked only 24th worldwide in the 100-meter breast stroke in 1991. Now he would be competing against the world's top swimmers.

On the night of July 26, eight swimmers stood on the apron of Barcelona's Picornell Swimming Stadium, ready for the 100-meter breast stroke. Norbert Rózsa of Hungary, the current world-record holder, was just one of the formidable competitors. Yet as the swimmers loosened up, Nelson appeared calm and focused, while the others shook their arms nervously and eyed one another warily. *Everybody here is scared,* Chris Martin thought, watching from the stands, *except Nelson!*

At the starting gun, Dmitry Volkov of the former U.S.S.R.'s Unified Team was off the blocks first. Next came Rózsa, then Vasily Ivanov, also of the Unified Team. Nelson, in lane three between Volkov and Ivanov, was keeping pace. At the turn, Nelson began to move past Ivanov. Then, in the last 15 meters, Nelson shot past Volkov and Rózsa into the lead. The others tried to catch him, but it was too late. Nelson finished in 1:01.50, an Olympic record.

Minutes later, Nelson Diebel stood on the victory stand, the gold medal around his neck, an Olympic champion at last. As "The Star-Spangled Banner" filled the night air, he suddenly started to cry. *I planned and dreamed and worked so hard,* he thought, *and I did it!*

Today, Nelson thinks often of Chris Martin, the man who believed in him when he didn't believe in himself. "The gold medal belongs as much to him as to me. If I do nothing else in life, I will try to give back to other kids what Chris Martin has given to me."

Never give out while there is hope.

WILLIAM PENN

NO GREATER LOVE

BY

JOHN PEKKANEN

$\mathcal{E}$rica Williams lay motionless in the darkened examining room as the technician moved the ultrasound transducer across her abdomen. "You're definitely pregnant," the technician announced. "You can see for yourself."

Erica looked closer at the tiny dot on the screen—the new life growing within her. She could barely contain her excitement.

Suddenly the technician's expression tightened. "What do you see?" Erica asked tensely.

"I just want to get a doctor to take a look," the woman answered.

Erica's mother, sitting nearby, squeezed her daughter's hand. "Please try not to worry," Virginia Van Wolvelaerd said. The torment, however, showed in the mother's eyes as well.

After examining the image, the doctor recommended that Erica consult with Audrey Richards, a gynecologist and obstetrician, who practiced near Erica's home in Micco on Florida's east coast. As they left, Erica turned to her mother. "It's back," she murmured. "I know it."

From earliest childhood, Erica had been raised in a close family that encouraged competition. She thrived on pitting herself against her two older brothers and one older sister. There were swimming races, fierce games of badminton and tennis. Erica usually accepted losing, yet she never gave in until the game was over. Above all, her family taught her always to face a problem squarely and do her best.

At age 17, Erica was found to have dysgerminoma, a rare ovarian cancer. Surgeons removed her right ovary and right Fallopian tube. Then, to kill any lingering cancer cells, her doctors recommended either radiation or chemotherapy. Radiation was the more proven therapy, but it would destroy Erica's remaining ovary—and her chance of ever having children. She decided to try chemotherapy.

Once her chemotherapy was completed, Erica's doctors were confident she had beaten the cancer. However, Erica was still haunted by the fear that she might never be a mother.

During the 1990 Christmas holidays, she missed her first period since the cancer treatment. She was 21 and newly married to Bob Williams, 33, a home-air-conditioning installer. In the course of their eight-month courtship, she had told Bob of her medical history. The chances were she'd never bear children, she said. So when the home pregnancy test came up positive, the couple was overjoyed.

Now, two weeks later, Erica and her mother sat nervously in Dr. Richards's office, awaiting the results of the ultrasound. "You are 6 1/2 weeks pregnant," Richards said softly, "but I'm afraid there's bad news too. We've detected a large mass in your left ovary. We can't be sure what it is."

Erica broke into sobs. "Will . . . my baby be all right?" she asked.

"I can't be sure at this point," Richards said.

Since Erica would require specialized care, Richards referred her to Dr. Linda Morgan at Shands Hospital in Gainesville, part of the

University of Florida School of Medicine. Morgan, director of the division of gynecologic oncology, had been one of Richards's teachers.

Bob and Erica drove to Gainesville later that week to meet with Dr. Morgan. A slender woman with a warm smile, Morgan inspired confidence. The couple liked her instantly. And almost from the moment she met Erica, Morgan knew this would be one of her special patients. Erica's bubbly, warm personality appealed to her, as did the young woman's vulnerability.

After examining Erica's medical records and ultrasound results, Morgan had no doubt that Erica's cancer had returned. Gently, she explained to Erica that the best way to save her life was to remove the cancerous ovary immediately. Again, the more proven follow-up treatment would be radiation. "Combined with surgery, this will give you a 90-percent chance of a full recovery." It also would mean the end of Erica's pregnancy.

"I know you're telling me what is medically best for me," Erica said finally, "but this is the only child I will ever be able to have. Isn't there some way I can be treated and not lose my baby? I'm willing to take risks for myself."

Another possibility, Morgan replied, would be to remove the ovary at 12 weeks of gestation—when the fetus would have a better chance of surviving the surgery—and withhold follow-up treatment until about the seventh month of pregnancy. Then the infant could be born by Caesarean section, and Erica's radiation treatment could begin. But this hinged on the hope that the cancer did not spread during that period. If it did, Morgan explained, Erica would be in grave danger.

"Could she die?" Bob asked.

"There's always that chance," said Morgan, "no matter what we do."

Bob's teeth clamped down on his tongue so hard that it started to bleed.

Erica felt torn. "What would you do?" she asked Morgan.

As a doctor, Morgan had already given her advice: remove the cancerous ovary and give Erica every chance she could. Putting herself in the young woman's shoes, though, Morgan knew her choice would be different. "I'd wait and see," she said. "It's a risk, but it's worth taking."

Erica had one more question.

"Do you believe in God?" she asked.

"Of course I do," Morgan answered. "I deliver babies."

That's all I wanted to hear, Erica thought.

"I have faith in you and in God, so let's wait," Erica said.

Bob had been raised a Baptist, but had not been to church in years. Soon after they married, however, Erica persuaded him to attend services with her and her parents at the Community Baptist Church in nearby Roseland. He could see that Erica's faith was a source of strength for her.

In February, the couple returned to Shands Hospital for Erica's surgery. She went into the operating room late in the morning on Valentine's Day. Exposing the affected area, Dr. Morgan saw that the dysgerminoma had totally invaded and twisted the ovary. It seemed miraculous that Erica had been able to get pregnant at all.

Probing gently, Morgan cut away the cancerous ovary and Fallopian tube, as well as some lymph nodes; these went for biopsy.

As Erica emerged from the anesthesia, she asked, "Is my baby okay?"

"Doing beautifully," Morgan assured her. Erica smiled and drifted back to sleep.

Later that afternoon, Morgan entered Erica's room and took her hand. "Your cancer has spread," the doctor said. The pathology lab had

. . . Now hope that is seen is not hope. For who hopes for what he sees? But if we hope for what we do not see, we wait for it with patience.

ROMANS 8

183

found it in her lymph nodes. "I'm terribly sorry, but we can't hold back treatment any longer."

Morgan felt that the only possibility for saving the baby—and Erica—was chemotherapy. This might put Erica at even higher risk, since chemotherapy was the less proven treatment for dysgerminoma. The baby would also be at risk, because chemotherapy attacks the body's most rapidly dividing cells—including those of a fetus. If any of these toxic drugs were to cross the placenta and reach the baby, Morgan realized, there was no telling the damage they might do.

Erica remained unwavering. "Do everything you can to save my baby," she pleaded.

Five days after surgery, Erica began a four-month regimen of chemotherapy. Morgan had sought to find drugs that would not harm Erica's baby. Each week-long treatment session in the hospital was followed by two weeks of recovery at home. Even with anti-nausea medication, she was violently ill. Bob helped Erica to the bathroom, cleaned up after her, massaged her back and hugged her. "We pledged to love one another in sickness and in health," he would remind her.

A stream of visitors poured through Erica's hospital room: family, friends and members of their church. They often joined Erica in prayer. With everyone, Erica fought to keep a happy face.

"Is it a boy or a girl?" Erica asked the ultrasound technicians one day. They couldn't be sure, but suspected a girl. After this, Erica referred to the baby as "she."

It was only at night, with Bob, that Erica's cheerful expression gave way to her darkest fears. "I could never get through this without you," she told Bob one evening as he gently stroked her neck and head. "But if I don't make it, and our baby survives, tell her how much I loved her, and how much I wanted her. Don't let her forget me."

In mid-May, 24 weeks into Erica's pregnancy, Dr. Morgan wanted to do a follow-up ultrasound of the baby. Erica watched closely as images flickered on the monitor. Her baby's human shape was clearly visible now. Seeing that picture of the life growing within her filled her with intense joy.

Then, suddenly, a white-colored mass loomed ominously on the screen, not far from her baby. "What's that?" she blurted, terrified.

"I'm not sure," Morgan told her. "It may be a tumor. Or it might be a benign growth, possibly a cyst."

For the first time, Erica's optimism almost dissolved. *I can feel her moving inside me*, she thought. *I can't lose her now!*

At 24 weeks, the baby was still 16 weeks away from full-term. They could wait another four weeks to see what happened to the mass, Morgan said. At that point the child might survive outside the womb. This was Erica's slender thread of hope.

During the long drive home, Bob kept his arm around Erica. "Maybe," he said, "God sent this little angel to you to let you know you were ill, so he could save your life. Maybe that was his purpose." *And if this baby does nothing more than save Erica's life*, Bob thought, *that's all I could ask for.*

Erica was not ready to give up, however. Sustaining her was an absolute trust in Dr. Morgan. *If anyone on this earth can get us through this ordeal*, Erica thought, *she can.*

On June 8—Bob's birthday—the couple finally had cause to celebrate. Erica's four months of chemotherapy was over. Follow-up tests showed no change in the mysterious mass. Dr. Morgan was encouraged.

Back home, Erica continued to have regular ultrasound scans. At the end of July, she underwent a series of tests—called a biophysical profile—to determine the well-being of the fetus. During the exam, she saw a worried look cloud the technician's face. "I know something's wrong," she said. "Is my baby okay?"

For the answer, Erica had to see Dr. Richards, who had continued to act as her regular obstetrician. "Your baby doesn't appear to be growing well," Dr. Richards said. "She may need to be delivered soon. I think you should go to Shands Hospital as soon as possible."

Within an hour, Erica, Bob and her mother were speeding toward Gainesville. Dr. Morgan immediately put Erica in the delivery suite and attached her to a fetal monitor. The baby was now 36 weeks old, a month premature, and not moving very much. This, the doctor explained, might indicate that the fetus was not getting enough oxygen.

Holding Erica's hand, Bob kept repeating, "Everything's going to be okay. It's going to work out." But after midnight, the baby's condition still hadn't improved.

"I think she'll do better if we get her out," Morgan said.

"Then please," Erica answered, "let's do it."

The Caesarean procedure went smoothly. At 4:20 a.m. on July 30, 1991, Erica gave birth to a three-pound, 14-ounce daughter. Immediately, Morgan looked for signs of abnormality. Certainly, the baby was small—partly the effect of chemotherapy. But when she screamed and wiggled her arms and legs, Morgan was ecstatic. *She's normal!*

The doctor then turned her attention to removing the white mass in Erica's pelvic region. On inspection, it was clearly a benign cyst. But that didn't mean Erica was free of cancer. Morgan removed some lymph nodes for lab study—and hoped.

Youth fades, love droops, the leaves of friendship fall. A mother's secret hope outlives them all.

OLIVER WENDELL HOLMES

That afternoon, Erica held her child for the first time. No longer could she hold back the tears and the flood of emotion that had built up for months.

The baby was taken to the Neo-natal Intensive Care Unit. When Bob was not at Erica's bedside, he'd go to the unit and insist on feeding his daughter—who bore a strong resemblance to him. Wanting to dress her up, he went to a toy store and bought clothing for Cabbage Patch dolls—a perfect fit.

Erica and her family now waited nervously for the pathology report. Definitive results would take a few days of lab work.

Five days after the baby's birth, Morgan hurried into Erica's room, beaming. "Good news!" she said. "There's no sign of cancer anywhere."

Bob and Erica's mother and father rushed to hug Erica. Then everyone turned and hugged Dr. Morgan. All shared tears of joy, including Linda Morgan.

Six months after the baby was born, Erica returned to Gainesville with her young daughter. This time, they visited Dr. Morgan at her home. As the two women embraced, all the fears and pain of the past seemed to dissolve.

The doctor held the little girl in her arms. "Look at how big you've grown," she whispered.

"Ten pounds now!" Erica said.

When it came time to leave, Erica said, "You'll always be a part of us." She and Bob knew they would never forget her. In the doctor's honor, they had christened their daughter Morgan Ashley Williams.

Linda Morgan smiled down at her namesake and gently kissed her good-by.

On the left margin (decorative handwritten text, vertical):

Yesterday seems less painful, and I am not afraid of tomorrow

WHY DO BAD THINGS HAPPEN TO GOOD PEOPLE?

BY

HAROLD S. KUSHNER

Our son, Aaron, a bright and happy child who could identify a dozen varieties of dinosaur, had just passed his third birthday. My wife and I had been concerned about his health because he stopped gaining weight at the age of eight months, and a few months later his hair started falling out. Yet prominent doctors had told us that, while Aaron would be very short as an adult, he would be normal in all other ways.

When we moved from New York to a Boston suburb, we discovered a pediatrician who was doing research in problems of children's growth. We introduced him to Aaron. Two months later he told us that our son's condition was called progeria, rapid aging. He said that Aaron would never grow much beyond three feet in height, would have no hair on his head or body, would look like a little old man while he was still a child, and would die in his early teens.

How does one handle such news? What I felt was a deep, aching sense of unfairness. I had been a good person. I had tried to do what was right. I was living a more religiously committed life than most people I knew. How could this happen to me?

Even if I deserved this punishment, on what grounds did an innocent child have to suffer? Why should he have to endure physical and psychological pain every day of his life? Why should he be condemned to grow into adolescence, see other boys and girls dating, and realize that he would never know marriage or fatherhood? It simply didn't make sense.

Why do bad things happen to good people? Virtually every conversation I have had on the subject of God and religion has gotten around to this question. The misfortunes of good people are a problem to everyone who wants to believe in a just and fair world.

I try to help my congregation of 2500 through the wrenching pain of their divorces, their business failures, their unhappiness with their children. But time and again, I have seen the wrong people get sick, the wrong people be hurt, the wrong people die young.

I was once called on to help a family through an almost unbearable tragedy. This middle-aged couple had one daughter, a bright 19-year-old college freshman. One morning they received a phone call from the university infirmary: "We have bad news. Your daughter collapsed while walking to class. A blood vessel burst in her brain, and she died before we could do anything. We're terribly sorry...."

I went over to see them that same day. I expected anger, shock, grief, but I didn't anticipate their first words: "You know, Rabbi, we didn't fast last Yom Kippur."

Why did they think that they were somehow responsible for this tragedy? Who taught them to believe in a God who would strike down a gifted young woman as punishment for someone else's ritual infraction?

Assuming that somehow our misfortunes come as punishment for our misdeeds is one way to make sense of the world's suffering. But such an answer has serious limitations. It creates guilt where there is no basis for guilt.

Yesterday seems less painful, and I am not afraid of tomorrow

Often, victims of misfortune try to console themselves with the idea that God has reasons that they are in no position to judge. I think of a woman I know named Helen.

She noticed herself getting tired easily. She chalked it up to getting older. Then one night, she stumbled over the threshold of her front door. The following morning, Helen made an appointment to see a doctor.

The diagnosis was multiple sclerosis, a degenerative nerve disease. The doctor explained that Helen might find it progressively harder to walk without support. Eventually she might be confined to a wheelchair, and become more and more of an invalid until she died.

Upon hearing the news, Helen broke down and cried: "I have a husband and young children who need me. I have tried to be a good person. I don't deserve this."

Her husband attempted to console her: "God must have his reasons for doing this, and it's not for us to question him. You have to believe that if he wants you to get better, you will, and if he doesn't, there has to be some purpose to it."

Helen wanted to be comforted by the knowledge that there was some purpose to her suffering, but her husband's words only made her feel more abandoned and more bewildered. What kind of higher purpose could possibly justify what she would have to face?

We have all read stories of little children who were left unwatched for just a moment and fell from a window or into a swimming pool and died. Why does God permit such things to happen? Is it to teach parents to be more careful? That is too trivial a lesson to be purchased at the price of a child's life. Is it to make the parents more sensitive, more compassionate people? The price is still too high.

Well, then, is tragedy a test? I was the parent of a handicapped child for 14 years, until his death. I was not comforted by the notion that God had singled me out because he recognized some special spiritual strength within me. I may be a more effective pastor, a more sympathetic counselor than I would ever have been without Aaron's death, but I would give up all those gains in a moment if I could have my son back.

Does God then "temper the wind to the shorn lamb"? Does he never ask more of us than we can endure? My experience has been otherwise. I have seen people crack under the strain of tragedy. I have seen marriages break up after the death of a child. I have seen people made noble and sensitive through suffering, but I have also seen people grow cynical and bitter. If God is testing us, he must know by now that many of us fail the test.

These various responses to tragedy all assume that God is the cause our suffering. But maybe our suffering happens for some reason other than the will of God. The Psalmist writes, "I will lift up mine eyes unto the hills, from whence cometh my help. My help cometh from the Lord, which made heaven and earth." He does not say "My tragedy comes from the Lord."

Could it be that God does not cause the bad things that happen to us? Could it be that he does not decide which families shall give birth to handicapped children but, rather, that he stands ready to help us cope with our tragedies?

One day, a year and a half after Aaron's death, I realized that I had gone beyond self-pity to accepting what had happened. I knew that no one ever promised us a life free from disappointment. The most anyone promised was that we would not be alone in our pain, that we would be able to draw upon a source outside ourselves for strength and courage.

I now recognize that God does not cause our misfortunes, but helps us—by inspiring other people to help. We were sustained in Aaron's illness by people who made a point of showing that they cared: the man who made Aaron a scaled-down tennis racket; the woman who gave him a small handmade violin; the friend who got him a baseball autographed by the Boston Red Sox; the children who overlooked his limitations to play stickball with him. These people were God's way of telling our family that we were not alone.

In the same way, I believe that Aaron served God's purposes, not by being sick but by facing up so bravely to his illness. Aaron's friends and schoolmates were affected by his courage and by the way he managed to live a full life despite his limitations. Others who knew our family were moved to handle the difficult times of their own lives with more hope and courage by our example.

Let me suggest that the bad things that happen to us in our lives do not have a meaning when they happen. But we can redeem these tragedies from senselessness by imposing meaning on them. In the final analysis, the question is not why bad things happen to good people, but how we respond when such things happen. Are we capable of accepting a world that has disappointed us by not being perfect, a world in which there is so much unfairness and cruelty, disease and crime, earthquake and accident? Are we capable of forgiving and loving the people around us, even if they have let us down? Are we capable of forgiving and loving God despite his limitations?

If we can do these things, we will be able to recognize that forgiveness and love are the weapons God has given to enable us to live fully and bravely in this less-than-perfect world.

I think of Aaron and all that his life taught me, and I realize how much I have lost and how much I have gained. Yesterday seems less painful, and I am not afraid of tomorrow.

I wait for the Lord, my soul waits,

and in his word I hope.

PSALM 130

THE PRICE OF LOVE

BY
FRED BAUER

If only I could keep the kids from naming him. That would be the trick.

"No family needs two dogs," I began dogmatically. And so I invoked the Bauer Anonymity Rule (BAR), which prohibits the naming of any animal not on the endangered-species list. That includes anything that walks or squawks, sings or swims, hops, crawls, flies or yodels, because at our place a pet named is a pet claimed.

"But we gotta call him something," our four children protested.

"All right, then, call him Dog X," I suggested. They frowned, but I thought it the perfect handle for something I hoped would float away like a generic soap powder.

My no-name strategy proved a dismal failure, however. Long before the pup was weaned, the kids secretly began calling him Scampy, and before I knew it he had become as much a fixture as the fireplace. And just as immovable.

All of this could have been avoided, I fumed, if Andy, a neighborhood mutt, had only stayed on his side of the street. But at age 14, this scruffy, arthritic mongrel hobbled into our yard for a tête-â-tête with our blue-blooded schnauzer, Baroness Heidi of Princeton on her AKC papers, who was a ten-year Old Maid. Before one could say "safe sex," we had a miracle of Sarah and Abraham proportions.

We were unaware that Andy had left his calling card until the middle of one night during our spring vacation in Florida. I thought the moaning noise was the ocean. But investigation revealed it was coming from Heidi, whom Shirley, my wife, pronounced in labor. "I *thought* she was getting fat," I mumbled sleepily.

When morning brought no relief or delivery, we found a vet who informed us that a big pup was blocking the birth canal, which could be fatal to Heidi. We wrung our hands for the rest of the day, phoning every couple of hours for an update. Not until evening was our dog pronounced out of danger.

"She was carrying three," the doctor reported, "but only one survived." The kids took one look at the male pup, a ragamuffin ball of string — red string, brown string, black string, tan string, gray string — and exclaimed, "Andy! He looks just like Andy." And there was no mistaking the father. Heidi's only genetic contribution seemed to be his schnauzer beard. Otherwise, he was an eclectic mix of terrier, collie, beagle, setter and Studebaker.

"Have you ever seen anything so homely?" I asked Shirley.

"He's adorable," she answered, admiringly. Too admiringly.

"I only hope someone else thinks so. His days with us are numbered." But I might as well have saved my breath. By the time Dog X reached ten weeks, our kids were more attached to him than barnacles to a boat's bottom. I tried to ignore him.

"Look at how good he is catching a ball, Dad," Christopher pointed out. I grunted noncommittally. And when Andy's folly performed his tricks — sit, fetch, roll over, play dead — and the kids touted his smarts, I hid behind a newspaper.

One thing I could not deny: he had the ears of a watchdog, detecting every sound that came from the driveway or yard. Heidi, his aging mother, heard nothing but his barking, which interrupted her frequent naps. He, on the other hand, was in perpetual motion. When the kids went off on their bikes or I put on my jogging shoes, he wanted to go along. If left behind, he chased squirrels. Occasionally, by now, I slipped and called him Scampy.

Then in the fall, after six months of family nurture and adoration, Scampy suffered a setback. Squealing brakes announced he had chased one too many squirrels into the street. The accident fractured his left hind leg, which the vet put in a splint. We were all relieved to hear his prognosis: complete recovery. But then a week later the second shoe dropped.

"Gangrene," Shirley told me one evening. "The vet says amputate or he'll have to be put to sleep." I slumped down in a chair.

"There's little choice," I said. "It's not fair to make an active dog like Scampy struggle around on three legs the rest of his life." Suddenly the kids, who had been eavesdropping, flew into the room.

"They don't kill a person who has a bad leg," Steve and Laraine argued.

Buying time, I told them, "We'll decide tomorrow." After the kids were in bed, Shirley and I talked.

"It will be hard for them to give up Scampy," she sympathized.

"Especially Christopher," I replied. "I was about his age when I lost Queenie." Then I told her about my favorite dog, a statuesque white spitz whose fluffy coat rolled like ocean waves when she ran. But Queenie developed a crippling problem with her back legs, and finally my dad said she would have to be put down.

"But she can get well," I pleaded. I prayed with all my might that God would help her walk again. But she got worse.

One night after dinner I went to the basement, where she slept beside the furnace. At the bottom of the stairs, I met Dad. His face was drained of color, and he carried a strange, strong-smelling rag in his hand.

"I'm sorry, but Queenie's dead," he told me gently. I broke into tears and threw myself into his arms. I don't know how long I sobbed, but after a while I became aware he was crying too. I remember how pleased I was to learn he felt the same way.

Between eye-wiping and nose-blowing, I told him, "I don't ever want another dog. It hurts too much when they die."

"You're right about the hurt, son," he answered, "but that's the price of love."

The next day, after conferring with the vet and the family, I reluctantly agreed to have Scampy's leg amputated. "If a child's faith can make him well," I remarked to Shirley, "then he'll recover four times over." And he did. Miraculously.

If I needed any proof that he was his old self, it came a short time after his operation. Watching from the kitchen window, I saw a fat gray squirrel creep toward the bird feeder. Slowly the sunning dog pulled himself into attack position. When the squirrel got to within a dozen feet, Scampy launched himself. Using his hind leg like a pogo stick, he rocketed into the yard and gave one bushy-tail the scare of its life.

Soon Scampy was back catching balls, tagging along with the kids, running with me as I jogged. The remarkable thing was the way he compensated for his missing appendage. He invented a new stroke for his lone rear leg, moving it piston-like from side to side to achieve both power and stability.

His enthusiasm and energy suffered no loss. "The best thing about Scampy," a neighbor said, "is that he doesn't know he's got a handicap. Either that or he ignores it, which is the best way for all of us to deal with such things."

Not that everyone saw him in a positive light. On the playground, some youngsters reacted as if he were a candidate for a Stephen King horror flick. "Look out," shouted one boy, "here comes Monster Dog!" Tripod and Hopalong were other tags. Our kids laughed off his detractors and introduced him as "Scampy, the greatest three-legged dog in the world."

For better than five years, Scampy gave us an object lesson in courage, demonstrating what it means to do your best with what you've got. On our daily runs I often carried on conversations with him as if he understood every word. "I almost shipped you out as a pup," I'd recount to him, "but the kids wouldn't let me. They knew how wonderful you were." It was obvious from the way he studied my face and wagged his tail that he liked to hear how special he was.

He probably would have continued to strut his stuff for a lot longer had he been less combative. In scraps in which he was clearly overmatched, he lacked two essentials for longevity — discretion and, partly because of his surgery, an effective reverse gear.

One warm August night he didn't return at his normal time, and the next morning he showed up, gasping for air and bloody around the neck. He obviously had been in a fight, and I suspected a badly damaged windpipe or lung.

"Scampy, when will you learn?" I asked as I petted his head. He looked up at me with those trusting eyes and licked my hand, but he was too weak to wag his tail. Christopher and Daniel helped me sponge him down and get him to the vet, but my diagnosis proved too accurate. By midday "the greatest three-legged dog in the world" was gone.

That evening Christopher and I drove to the vet's office, gathered up the black plastic bag that held Scampy and headed home. Scampy's mother, Heidi, had died at 15 a few months before; now we would bury him next to her in the woods by the garden.

As we drove, I tried to engage Christopher in conversation, but he was silent, apparently sorting through his feelings. "I've seen lots of dogs, Christopher," I said, "but Scampy was something special."

"Yep," he answered, staring into the darkness.

"He was certainly one of the smartest." Christopher didn't answer. From flashes of light that passed through the car I could see him dabbing his eyes. Finally he looked at me and spoke.

"There's only one thing I'm sure of, Dad," he choked out through tears. "I don't want another dog. It feels so bad to lose them."

"Yes, I know," I said. Then, drawing on a voice and words that were not my own, I added, "But that's the price of love."

Now his sobs were audible, and I was having trouble seeing the road myself. I pulled off at a service station and stopped the car. There, I put my arms around him and with my tears let him know — just as my father had shown me — that his loss was my loss too.

Even now I am full of hope, but the end lies in God.

PINDAR

MY FATHER'S MUSIC

BY

WAYNE KALYN

I remember the day Dad first lugged the heavy accordion up our front stoop, taxing his small frame. He gathered my mother and me in the living room and opened the case as if it were a treasure chest. "Here it is," he said. "Once you learn to play, it'll stay with you for life."

If my thin smile didn't match his full-fledged grin, it was because I had prayed for a guitar or a piano. It was 1960, and I was glued to my AM radio, listening to Del Shannon and Chubby Checker. Accordions were nowhere in my hit parade. As I looked at the shiny white keys and cream-colored bellows, I could already hear my friends' squeeze-box jokes.

For the next two weeks, the accordion was stored in the hall closet. Then one evening Dad announced that I would start lessons the following week. In disbelief I shot my eyes toward Mom for support. The firm set of her jaw told me I was out of luck.

Spending $300 for an accordion and $5 per lesson was out of character for my father. He was practical always — something he learned growing up on a Pennsylvania farm. Clothes, heat and sometimes even food were scarce.

Before I was born, he and my mother moved into her parents' two-story home in Jersey City, N.J. I grew up there on the second floor; my grandparents lived downstairs. Each weekday Dad made the three-hour commute to and from Long Island, where he was a supervisor in a company that serviced jet engines. Weekends, he tinkered in the cellar, turning scraps of plywood into a utility cabinet or fixing a broken toy with spare parts. Quiet and shy, he was never more comfortable than when at his workbench.

Only music carried Dad away from his world of tools and projects. On a Sunday drive, he turned the radio on immediately. At red lights, I'd notice his foot tapping in time. He seemed to hang on every note.

Still, I wasn't prepared when, rummaging in a closet, I found a case that looked to me like a tiny guitar's. Opening it, I saw the polished glow of a beautiful violin. "It's your father's," Mom said. "His parents bought it for him. I guess he got too busy on the farm to ever learn to play it." I tried to imagine Dad's rough hands on this delicate instrument — and couldn't.

Shortly after, my lessons began with Mr. Zelli at the Allegro Accordion School, tucked between an old movie theater and a pizza parlor. On my first day, with straps straining my shoulders, I felt clumsy in every way. "How did he do?" my father asked when it was over. "Fine for the first lesson," said Mr. Zelli. Dad glowed with hope.

I was ordered to practice half an hour every day, and every day I tried to get out of it. My future seemed to be outside playing ball, not in the house mastering songs I would soon forget. But my parents hounded me to practice.

Gradually, to my surprise, I was able to string notes together and coordinate my hands to play simple songs. Often, after supper, my father would request a tune or two. As he sat in his easy chair, I would fumble through "Lady of Spain" and "Beer Barrel Polka."

"Very nice, better than last week," he'd say. Then I would segue into a medley of his favorites, "Red River Valley" and "Home on the Range," and he would drift off to sleep, the newspaper folded on his lap. I took it as a compliment that he could relax under the spell of my playing.

One July evening I was giving an almost flawless rendition of "Come Back to Sorrento," and my parents called me to an open window. An elderly neighbor, rarely seen outside her house, was leaning against our car humming dreamily to the tune. When I finished, she smiled broadly and called out, "I remember that song as a child in Italy. Beautiful, just beautiful."

Throughout the summer, Mr. Zelli's lessons grew more difficult. It took me a week and a half to master them now. All the while I could hear my buddies outside playing heated games of stickball. I'd also hear an occasional taunt: "Hey, where's your monkey and cup?"

Such humiliation paled, though, beside the impending fall recital. I would have to play a solo on a local movie theater's stage. I wanted to skip the whole thing. Emotions boiled over in the car one Sunday afternoon.

"I don't want to play a solo," I said.

"You have to," replied my father.

"Why?" I shouted. "Because you didn't get to play your violin when you were a kid? Why should I have to play this stupid instrument when you never had to play yours?"

Dad pulled the car over and pointed at me.

"Because you can bring people joy. You can touch their hearts. That's a gift I won't let you throw away." He added softly, "Someday you'll have the chance I never had: you'll play beautiful music for your family. And you'll understand why you've worked so hard."

I was speechless. I had rarely heard Dad speak with such feeling about anything, much less the accordion. From then on, I practiced without my parents' making me.

The evening of the concert Mom wore glittery earrings and more makeup than I could remember. Dad got out of work early, put on a suit and tie, and slicked down his hair with Vitalis. They were ready an hour early, so we sat in the living room chatting nervously. I got the unspoken message that playing this one song was a dream come true for them.

At the theater nervousness overtook me as I realized how much I wanted to make my parents proud. Finally, it was my turn. I walked to the lone chair on stage and performed "Are You Lonesome Tonight?" without a mistake. The applause spilled out, with a few hands still clapping after others had stopped. I was light-headed, glad my ordeal was over.

After the concert Mom and Dad came backstage. The way they walked — heads high, faces flushed — I knew they were pleased. My mother gave me a big hug. Dad slipped an arm around me and held me close. "You were just great," he said. Then he shook my hand and was slow to let it go.

As the years went by, the accordion drifted to the background of my life. Dad asked me to play at family occasions, but the lessons stopped. When I went to college, the accordion stayed behind in the hall closet next to my father's violin.

A year after my graduation, my parents moved to a house in a nearby town. Dad, at 51, finally owned his own home. On moving day, I didn't have the heart to tell him he could dispose of the accordion, so I brought it to my own home and put it in the attic.

There it remained, a dusty memory, until one afternoon several years later when my two children discovered it by accident. Scott thought it was a secret treasure; Holly thought a ghost lived inside. They were both right.

When I opened the case, they laughed and said, "Play it, play it." Reluctantly, I strapped on the accordion and played some simple songs. I was surprised my skills hadn't rusted away. Soon the kids were dancing in circles and giggling. Even my wife, Terri, was laughing and clapping to the beat. I was amazed at their unbridled glee.

My father's words came back to me: "Someday you'll have the chance I never had. Then you'll understand."

I finally knew what it meant to work hard and sacrifice for others. Dad had been right all along: the most precious gift is to touch the hearts of those you love.

Later I phoned Dad to let him know that, at long last, I understood. Fumbling for the right words, I thanked him for the legacy it took almost 30 years to discover. "You're welcome," he said, his voice choked with emotion.

Dad never learned to coax sweet sounds from his violin. Yet he was wrong to think he would never play for his family. On that wonderful evening, as my wife and children laughed and danced, they heard my accordion. But it was my father's music.

Hope is like the sun, which, as
we journey towards it, casts the
shadow of our burden behind us.

SAMUEL SMILES

MY SAMARITAN EXPERIMENT

BY

JOHN SHERRILL

One hot August afternoon several years ago, my wife Tib and I were driving along I-75 in south Florida when the red square with a picture of a watering can began to glow on the dashboard. I pulled off the road and opened the hood. Through the steam rising from the engine I could see that the wheel that drives the fan belt had flown apart.

Tib and I stood in the glare of the sun, looking down the lonely stretch of highway. The last big overhead sign had said "Next Exit: 40 Miles," and I had no idea how far we'd come since then. I did know that even a few miles would be too far to walk in this heat.

A cluster of cars went by; no one even slowed. Maybe they were afraid to. A rash of highway robberies had recently made headlines in southern Florida. We stood beside our automobile as cars passed. I quit counting at 100.

Finally, an hour and a half later, a pickup braked as it went by. I saw its turn signal, and when it pulled onto the shoulder I ran toward it. The driver, probably in his 30s, wore overalls caked with gray mud.

"Problemas?" the young farmer asked. He spoke about as much English as I do Spanish.

The man walked back to our car, looked under the hood and shook his head. With sign language—pointing to us, then to his truck—he indicated he'd take us to find help. So we got into the pickup. To see out the mud-splattered windshield, I had to look past a crucifix dangling from the mirror.

The farmer took the first exit, 20 miles down the road. It was another five miles to the nearest town. At the garage he waited to be sure we were being looked after, then headed for his truck. I pulled out my wallet to pay him for his trouble. He shook his head. So we exchanged handshakes, and he was gone.

Before nightfall we were on our way, still giving thanks for our good Samaritan. "How do you repay a kindness like that?" I asked.

"We can't," Tib said. "But maybe we can pass it along."

Pass it along! Of course. "I'm going to stop and help another driver stuck on a highway somewhere," I declared. But that seemed so little. "No, not *one* driver," I said. "I'm going to help ten!"

Forming that high-minded resolve was one thing; acting on it was another. Like most people, I always seemed to be in a hurry. The next few times I saw a car beside the road, someone was waiting for me at the other end, so I didn't stop. On another occasion, I suddenly became acutely aware of my own vulnerability—after all, there *were* angry and deranged people out there. Clearly, I had to be careful. As I drove on, I asked God to guide me.

Soon after, Tib and I were driving through rural New Jersey when we passed a family stopped beside the road—a man, a woman and two youngsters. Both the father and the little boy were wearing yarmulkes.

Tib and I exchanged nods.

The embarrassed man told us they'd run out of gas. As we drove him to a filling station, we told him the story of our Florida Samaritan.

That night, when Tib and I were unpacking the car, we found the man's wallet on the floor of the back seat. I called to say I'd send it by certified mail in the morning.

"I hope you weren't worried," I added.

"Of course not. Would the good Samaritan steal?"

Since then I have stopped for breakdowns in half a dozen states.

Being a Samaritan has sometimes required a small expense—a couple of dollars for phone calls, or a cup of coffee. One day, driving through the outskirts of Charleston, S.C., I passed a truck filled with produce, stalled at curbside with its hood raised. A block farther I noticed a grizzled man trudging down the road, lugging a heavy auto part. I pulled over. "That your truck back there?"

The man put down his load. "This confounded starter motor again! If you can take me to the parts yard . . . "

As it turned out, he was a few dollars short of the price of the replacement part. A small amount—nothing compared with the smile that warmed me on my way after I'd driven him back to his truck.

Sometimes stopping has cost me time. Barreling along a California freeway one day, I passed an old car on the edge of the highway flying the standard signal of distress: a handkerchief tied to the antenna. A woman sat in the driver's seat.

I had to exit and backtrack in order to reach her. The round trip took 20 minutes, but the woman was still there, and she was crying.

"Don't mind me," she apologized. "I've been sitting here over an hour. I didn't know what to do."

I took extra time with her, driving her to a restaurant and waiting until the road-service people arrived. Over coffee I told her about our Florida experience. "Thank God for that farmer!" she said.

It's true. Because of that farmer, a minor chain reaction of kindness has started. For me, the biggest reward has been a shift in my own attitudes. Over the years I had become suspicious of people who are not my neighbors—people from another race, another generation or culture. It's well to be sensible, of course; we do live in a century of violence (as did the Biblical good Samaritan). But I want to side with those who say that most people are friendly, most are honest.

It has been years since I pulled over to help my first motorist-in-need. My tenth stop has long since been completed. But I wouldn't stop stopping for the world.

When Tib and I were driving along a levee above the Mississippi River, we came upon a young black woman in a station wagon full of children. They'd stopped for a picnic, and now her car wouldn't start. With our jumper cables I got her engine going. "How much?" she asked. In answer I told her about the farmer.

"I'm going to do it!" she exclaimed. "I'm going to help people just like you're doing!"

This mother's reaction to my story of the Florida Samaritan was typical. Some people admitted they'd be too scared to stop, but said they'd find some other way to help, such as calling the highway patrol at the next exit.

I am glad others want to keep the Samaritan chain intact. They may find, as I have, that the rewards far outweigh the time or expense it takes to help a stranger.

Hope is the thing with feathers
That perches in the soul,
And sings the tune without the words,
And never stops at all,

And sweetest in the gale is heard;
And sore must be the storm
That could abash the little bird
That kept so many warm.

I've heard it in the chillest land,
And on the strangest sea;
Yet, never, in extremity,
It asked a crumb of me.

EMILY DICKINSON

WINDOW
of HOPE

Special Feature

BY

KATIE MCCABE

JoAnne Johnson, her arms encircling the water-polo ball, sprinted toward the net at the end of the pool. But all at once her muscles gave way, and the other rookies on Brown University's water-polo club shot past her.

"Head up, shoulders out of the water!" the captain shouted in encouragement. Embarrassed that she could not keep up, JoAnne willed her arms to control the ball. Her muscles, though toned from years of competitive swimming, simply defied her. A dull, leaden sensation dragged at her legs. She reached for the edge of the pool and hung on, panting. "I don't know what's wrong with me," she told a teammate. "It's like I've got rocks in my arms."

Alone in the locker room, JoAnne collapsed on a bench and began toweling her long brown hair. Her mind played over what the nurse said the previous day when she had gone to Health Services complaining of fatigue. The nurse's eyes widened as JoAnne rattled off her schedule—intensive Russian, economics, calculus, history, a part-time job, political work, water polo, volleyball. In between, JoAnne admitted, she'd squeezed in a few midnight dorm parties.

213

"No wonder you're exhausted! We'll get blood work, but I wouldn't worry. Sounds to me like a case of freshman overload."

JoAnne might have believed that, had it not been for her bruises. At the gentlest poke, angry-looking splotches appeared under her skin. It was the reddish-yellow patch on her hip that really had her worried—it broke out after she had tumbled from a canoe almost a month ago. Instead of fading, the color was deepening and spreading.

JoAnne pulled her sweatshirt over her head and hurried out of the locker room. The biting October air cut through her weariness.

"I wouldn't have believed there could be a place like this," she had told her mom and dad on parents' weekend the previous Saturday. For JoAnne, a black honor student whose intellect and background had impressed her high-school teachers, Brown was more than a good school. It felt like home.

As JoAnne stepped off the elevator on the third floor of her dorm, the predictable chorus of voices greeted her. "We're waiting for you to teach us another one of your Russian dances," her friend Fara Wolfson said.

The week before, JoAnne had pulled her fellow freshmen into the hallway to demonstrate dances she was learning in her Russian class. One by one, she had conned the most reluctant bystanders into her chorus line. "Who says you have to be Russian to do this? My Russian prof is *Irish*," she had appealed.

Now someone, echoing JoAnne, called out, "Let us begin the national dance of —"

"Maybe another night, guys," JoAnne said, pushing open the door to her room. "I've got to hit the books. I won't even *pass* Russian if I don't get going. . . ."

Looks of surprise spread over their faces. JoAnne worried about passing? JoAnne tackled courses that had upperclassmen sweating. No one had ever heard her worry about homework. She just got it all done.

With exchanges of disappointed "Good night," her friends headed back to their rooms. JoAnne dropped on her bed, shoved her books to one side and shut her eyes. She'd been whipping through Russian tapes at the rate of three and four a day, relishing the novel sound of the language. Tonight, though, even Russian seemed unbearable.

She set her roommate's clock for 7 a.m. *I can't afford to oversleep again,* she thought. Twice in the last few days, she'd awakened to the sound of the ticking clock and the sickening realization that she'd slept through all her classes. Soon she'd be too far behind to catch up. *If I can just get a few hours' rest tonight,* she told herself, *I'll work double time tomorrow.*

The next day, October 26, 1988, JoAnne found that even double time was not enough. Somehow, she managed to make it to her classes and was now holed up in the study lounge, her head pounding at the sound of each Russian syllable on her grammar tape. As the kids began coming in from class, she tried to block out the noise of the greetings they shouted back and forth to one another.

Suddenly, out of the din, JoAnne heard her own name being called. She turned to see her roommate, Cheryl Anderson, standing in the lounge doorway, holding the phone out to her: "It's for you, Jo."

The voice on the other end was businesslike and unfamiliar. "JoAnne, this is Dr. Wheeler from Health Services. Your blood-test results came back sooner than we expected. Could you come down to talk with me this afternoon?"

Why had the doctor called so soon? JoAnne wondered. *And why did she have to go immediately?*

She spotted her friend April Wazeka in the next room, studying. "Hey, April, Health Services just phoned," she said. "They want me to come down right away."

April, looking up from her work, caught a look on JoAnne's face and offered to go along.

"I wonder if I'm coming down with the flu," JoAnne speculated as the two of them walked in the afternoon sunlight.

Then, as if determined to drive away the nagging worry, JoAnne launched into a review of eligible dating prospects from the previous weekend's party. Her contagious laugh echoed through the vestibule of the Health Center as the two young women entered the building and slipped into empty chairs in the waiting room.

JoAnne straightened up as the doctor called her name. She looked at his face, and her smile faded. "I just hope I don't have mono," she whispered to April as she got up to follow the doctor. "I absolutely cannot afford to miss any more classes!"

Dr. Wheeler looked down at a sheaf of papers, then up at JoAnne, sitting on the other side of his desk. "JoAnne, your blood test came back from the lab today."

"I wasn't expecting to hear so soon," JoAnne told him. "But I've been so tired, I knew there must be something wrong. What is it?"

"You have leukemia, JoAnne. An acute form of leukemia." The doctor paused. "We need to get you home. We don't have the facilities to take care of you here, and it's very important to get you started on treatment right away."

JoAnne began to cry. For several minutes, neither she nor Dr. Wheeler spoke. At last, JoAnne broke the silence. "Am I going to die?"

"There are treatments for leukemia," he explained. "Once the doctors determine what type of leukemia you have, they will put you on a regimen of chemotherapy."

Dr. Wheeler omitted numbers that had shocked him. JoAnne's white-cell count was 200,000 — 20 times higher than normal.

There was nothing you couldn't lick with facts and guts and prayers.

One look under the microscope at the immature "blast" cells signifying leukemia, and he had phoned JoAnne's pediatrician at Georgetown University Medical Center in Washington, D.C., to arrange for her immediate admission. A white-cell count of 200,000 could prove lethal if untreated. More ominously, her bone marrow was manufacturing leukemia cells very rapidly.

Dr. Wheeler voiced none of those concerns to JoAnne. Instead, he said that her pediatrician had been in touch with her parents. They had booked her on a six o'clock flight out of Providence that evening.

JoAnne, no longer tearful, cut to the bottom line: "When can I come back to Brown?"

"That depends on how quickly we can get your leukemia into remission," Wheeler replied. "Right now, let's concentrate on getting you home to the experts."

It was 8 p.m. when JoAnne's plane landed at Washington National Airport. Her backpack was stuffed with gifts from the kids at the dorm —a homemade card, a fistful of lollipops, a *Sesame Street Magazine* —"to keep your mind sharp," her friends said.

"Now you all quit getting so worked up," she had told them. "I'll be back by Thanksgiving!"

The worried faces of her friends were a blur now. JoAnne just wanted to go home — home to her dog, her friends, her brother Stephen, who could tease her out of the most serious mood. Most of all, she wanted to see her parents.

When JoAnne spotted her mother at the gate, she broke out into a smile. "Well, Mom, here I am!"

Sylvia Johnson, still reeling from the phone call that had turned her world upside down, smiled at her daughter's wry matter-of-factness. "Hi, precious! Daddy's waiting."

She studied her daughter's face. There was vulnerability and fear, but there was also a look she had seen a hundred times when JoAnne was poised at the start of a race. She could feel her daughter fortifying herself to do battle.

"JoAnne, we won't be going home," Sylvia Johnson said as they stood outside the airport, looking for their car. "The doctor at Georgetown insists you check in tonight. He wants to start you on antibiotics right away."

JoAnne's face fell, but she said nothing. There was her father, pulling up to the curb.

"Hi, sweetie pie! Let's get your bags."

JoAnne answered with a hug, then jumped into the back seat. As always, JoAnne provided her parents with a detailed report of everything that had happened. There had never been anything she couldn't share with them.

But tonight, for the first time, she left out the most important part —about the first terrible 15 minutes after the diagnosis. Over and over, she had repeated the same questions. "Leukemia? How can I have leukemia? Maybe they made a mistake. I just had a physical in August, and everything was fine. Leukemia is *cancer*. I can't believe I have cancer."

But her parents had taught her, from the time she was a little girl, that whining got you nowhere, that there was nothing you couldn't lick with facts and guts and prayer.

And her parents themselves had proved it—earning their Ph.D.s when JoAnne and her brother Stephen were babies, pinching pennies to give their kids music and skating and swimming lessons. When the family left the University of Iowa to come to Washington, JoAnne saw their careers take off—her mother as an education professor at Howard University, her father as director of counseling at a federal agency.

She'd watched her soft-spoken, scholarly parents analyze problems and attack them. JoAnne had done the same, grabbing everything they put before her, hungry for the next challenge—from her first swimming lesson to her admission to an Ivy League college. Until tonight, beating the odds had been easy.

The pediatric ward at Georgetown was quiet as Dr. Joseph E. Gootenberg walked in. JoAnne looked hard at this stocky, black-bearded young doctor who headed the hematology-oncology program. JoAnne sensed that the terrible news was about to get worse.

"In order to start treating the leukemia, we have to know precisely what kind it is," he told the Johnsons. "And we won't know until we see the results of the bone-marrow biopsy. Right now, we just have to make sure JoAnne is safe."

A nurse hooked up intravenous tubes and started to administer massive doses of antibiotics. JoAnne closed her eyes.

"Do you want me to stay with you tonight?" her mother asked.

"No, don't worry about me, Mom," JoAnne murmured sleepily. "I'll be okay."

"Acute biphenotypic leukemia." Dr. Gootenberg called it when at last, after three days of tests, he identified the diease. "Somewhere in JoAnne's bone marrow, the genetic makeup of a single cell changed. We have no idea what causes that to happen. It's as though one cell goes crazy. Then that mutant cell becomes leukemic, multiplies, and begins to crowd out normal cells. The mutant cells are very, very hard to kill."

"When can we begin treatment?" Howard Johnson asked.

"We'll put JoAnne on a chemotherapy regimen tomorrow morning," Dr. Gootenberg said. Then he leaned toward JoAnne. "You have a very vicious, complicated leukemia, JoAnne. In all probability, we can bring it into remission. But the chances are overwhelming that you will relapse. The prognosis is really very bad."

This was not the first time an adult had shaken his head as JoAnne tackled "the impossible"—a language teacher had told her she'd never master a year of Spanish and French on independent study; even Ronald Kearns, her high-school jazz instructor who believed she could do anything, had raised an eyebrow when she said she'd learn a bass part in three days. She'd proved them all wrong.

Now here stood this doctor, telling her she was going to be undone by one malformed cell in her bone marrow. The idea was ludicrous.

JoAnne stared at Dr. Gootenberg, who looked grim and intense, and she started to laugh.

Even JoAnne's parents, well acquainted with her stubborn optimism, were taken aback. Yet JoAnne, exhausted, lying in bed with a catheter implanted in her chest, had without a single word laid down Battle Rule No. 1: *Negativism Prohibited.*

But Dr. Gootenberg's grimmest warnings did not prepare JoAnne for what she faced the next morning: first, a numbing of the skin at the lower back; then, the insertion of the long needle into the spine; and finally, as the chemicals entered her bloodstream, waves of nausea and vomiting. And next the spinal headache began.

Sylvia Johnson, sitting at JoAnne's bedside, could not contain her anger. "I don't understand why this had to happen to you," she said, tears streaming down her face.

JoAnne turned her head on her pillow and took in her mother's rage.

"Mom, things happen to people. Horrible things happen to people all the time. What can you do?"

"But to *you*, JoAnne, *right now* . . ."

She broke off, but JoAnne knew the rest, the part her mother couldn't bring herself to say: ". . . just when you were about to do everything your father and I had ever imagined for you, and more . . ."

JoAnne broke into her mother's thoughts. "Hey, Mom, we'll handle it. I'll help you."

Her mother smiled. This was the wry, wise child who, one difficult summer years ago when money was tight, had found her mother mop-ing over bills and a stack of educational consulting work.

"Show me what you have to do," 11-year-old JoAnne had said to Sylvia, "and I'll help you." As her mother began analyzing standardized test questions, JoAnne sat listening, and challenging, and offering sug-gestions —and the two of them had gotten through it.

Sylvia told her daughter, as she had years ago, "JoAnne, I'm so glad I've got you to get me through this!"

Everyone but JoAnne, it seemed, wanted to know "Why?" — Stephen, her father, her friends. While everyone around her railed at the unfairness of her leukemia, JoAnne withdrew from questions. Even her pastor, Dean Louis Moe, long acquainted with the depth of her faith, was amazed by JoAnne's serenity.

"JoAnne, what are you feeling? Is there anything you want to talk about?" he probed, remembering how relentlessly she had questioned him about theology as a youngster.

"No," she told him, "I'd just like to pray with you."

Only her best friend, Natasha Rabchevsky, glimpsed what JoAnne struggled with so silently. The two sat in JoAnne's hospital room on a November weekend, speaking in French, as they had since high school, of the things they could talk about to no one else. Only a few weeks earlier, Natasha confided to JoAnne, her mother had been told she had cancer.

"I just don't understand," said JoAnne, "why this has to happen to people like your mother and me."

"JoAnne, my mother says she's lived her life, raised two kids, seen the world. But she keeps asking me, 'How can something like this happen to JoAnne? She's so young.'"

"Natash, to tell you the truth, I wanted to say that, but I didn't want

"I know he thinks I can't beat it Mom, but I know I can."

221

to sound as though what's happening to me is worse than what's happening to your mom. There's just so much I want to do. . . ."

Chatting on the phone with her Brown friends, JoAnne deflected questions about her treatment. The more brutal the drug regimen became, the less she spoke of it. When her beautiful long hair began to fall out in clumps on her pillow, JoAnne was silent.

The therapy that exhausted her and bloated her and made her bald was her ticket back to Brown. Remission was her goal. Strong, athletic, her heart and lungs in prime condition, she amazed Dr. Gootenberg with her tolerance for high-dose chemotherapy. Determined to puncture his pessimism, she matched each of his projections with one of her own.

"Just wait, Dr. G," she informed him in mid-November. "I'll be back at school before Christmas!"

"Unlikely," Gootenberg replied.

JoAnne rolled her eyes and whispered to her mother as Dr. Gootenberg left the room, "Dr. G — that's short for Dr. Gloom and Doom. I know he thinks I can't beat it, Mom, but I know I can."

Almost as abruptly as her leukemic cells had appeared, they began their retreat, disappearing under the drug onslaught. Barely three weeks into her treatment, Dr. Gootenberg came into her room, twinkling through his gruffness. "You're moving into remission much more quickly than we expected," he told her.

JoAnne's look said, "No more quickly than *I* expected!"

JoAnne's white-cell count edged toward normal. The moment she felt her energy returning, she moved into high gear. She phoned Brown to catch up on her friends and sent her father in search of a Russian tutor.

A few days before Thanksgiving, her parents walked into her room, beaming. "We just spoke with your friend Dr. Gloom," her father told her. "You are now in remission. You can come home."

An impish grin spread over JoAnne's face. "And then back to Brown," she said. She picked up the phone, dialed a friend at the dorm, and issued a volley of instructions.

What Dr. Gootenberg heard, however, as he phoned colleagues around the country about treatment, did not bode well for JoAnne's return to Brown.

JoAnne's shoulders sagged as she listened to her revised cancer protocol: stronger drugs, in higher doses, administered in complex and varying combinations. Dr. Gootenberg was unequivocal. The best shot against this leukemia was to wipe it out in the first round.

The bottom line was painfully obvious: JoAnne could forget about going back to Brown in January.

"When *can* I go back to school?"

"I'm afraid not for at least two years," Dr. Gootenberg replied.

JoAnne slumped in her chair. Her father, sitting next to her, reached out and took her hand.

For the first time, she had come up against something as relentless and unstoppable as she was. The leukemia, Dr. Gootenberg explained, would be even more vicious if it returned. Any mutant cells that survived the first assault of chemotherapy would undergo another mutation to make them harder to kill in their second life.

"Our best shot," said Dr. Gootenberg, "is to wipe them out completely, so there is no second round."

"And if that fails?" Howard Johnson asked.

"If that fails," Gootenberg said slowly, "there is another option. We can replace JoAnne's bone marrow with marrow from a healthy donor. That can be ideal if the body accepts the donor's marrow cells as its own. But it's horrific if it rejects them as foreign. And if the *marrow* recognizes the *body* as foreign, it launches an antibody attack on the patient. We call that graft versus host disease."

The trick was to fool the body into believing the new cells were its own, Dr. Gootenberg explained. Once they were engrafted into JoAnne's marrow, they would begin producing healthy cells. Everything turned on being able to find an exact genetic double of JoAnne. The best chance for a match was one of her blood relatives.

"What if we don't match?" Howard asked.

Then, Dr. Gootenberg said, they could turn to registries of unrelated donors—people who have had their blood typed to identify the group of proteins in the immune system that recognize and reject foreign tissue.

"Up until the past few years, we never tried to match these human leukocyte antigens, or HLAs, outside a person's own family," he explained. "But blood typing is more sophisticated now, and if the HLA match is good enough, the donor cells 'take' just as well as those from a blood relative. The tough part is finding the match."

The figures Dr. Gootenberg threw out sounded overwhelming: There were 26 million combinations of antigens. Finding a match usually required a search of 20,000 people. And you could search through two or three times that many —the size of the existing pool of U.S. donors—and not locate a match. It was, Dr. Gootenberg cautioned, "like looking for a needle in a haystack."

A few days later, on New Year's Eve, JoAnne arrived at a high-school friend's house ready to ring in 1989. Not even with her closest friends did she share the news that the ideal scenario of a family match had evaporated immediately. Her parents were only half-matches; because Stephen was adopted, he was not a candidate; a search of her relatives had been fruitless.

What JoAnne announced to her friends was her first-round victory. "I'm officially in remission now!" she told them. "I know you're insanely jealous of my Diana Ross look-alike wig," she said with mock seriousness, yanking off the synthetic wig to reveal her bald head.

Her friends couldn't help laughing. "You look gorgeous, Jo," Natasha said.

JoAnne was eager to relive the trip they'd all made to France, when they became so inseparable they'd named themselves "The Exclusive Obnoxious American French Foursome"—the EOAFFs.

Sprawled on the floor, they pored over photo albums of the three weeks when they took France by storm. JoAnne flipped to her favorite picture—the EOAFFs at a Paris pub.

"Well, *mes amies*, I can't drink beer now," JoAnne announced. "That's why I carry this handy flask filled with . . . vodka." Laughing, she pulled up her sweater to reveal the plastic pouch strapped to her waist. The bag filled with chemo drugs was connected to a portable pump. Without it, she would not have been able to leave the hospital.

The frightening game of genetic roulette that had begun that afternoon, with her mother contacting the American Registry for a donor search, was to JoAnne a remote "just in case." She had proved Dr. Gootenberg wrong once already. She had made up her mind that there would be no second round.

With a bounce punctuating her athletic walk, JoAnne strode into the pediatric oncology clinic of the Lombardi Cancer Center in January, ready to begin maintenance chemotherapy as an outpatient.

By now, she was used to the upside-down "triumphs" of leukemia treatment. Even the chemotherapy routine no longer upset her. The bizarre roller coaster began with endless waiting for pathology results, always hoping for a blood count high enough so she could withstand the next onslaught of drugs. The better her counts, the higher the drug doses—and the greater the pain and exhaustion.

What stopped her short were the other patients — every one of them as sick as she was, only much younger. Clustered around her as she sat in the waiting room, they handed her books, begged her to draw for them. JoAnne put aside her readings in French philosophy, and turned out sketches of clowns and rainbows.

What she had not prepared for, as she held her own cancer at bay, was watching the faces disappear from her eager circle. JoAnne sketched for them, told them stories, and, one by one, watched them die.

"They're so *little*," she told the oncology counselor after the deaths of two of the youngest children. But the death of a teen-age patient hit hardest of all. With her, JoAnne had waited for treatments, shared her feelings, talked of life after leukemia. "Why can't somebody *do something?*" JoAnne asked angrily. "I just wish there were something *I* could do."

JoAnne pitted her will against the disease with ferocity, refusing to allow it to derail her life. Even when her head ached so badly from spinal injections that she could hardly see, she sat through two-hour psychology lectures at Georgetown University, turned in French compositions, and made every performance of the campus jazz ensemble she'd joined.

Only JoAnne's family knew how, late at night, she wrestled with the reality of cancer. Unable to sleep, she struggled with her dread of self-administered chemotherapy. She'd stare at the floor, turning the needle in her hand, finally summoning her mother to give her the I.V. push through the catheter in her chest.

But the payoff came in her clinic visits; week in, week out, her slides were clean. The nagging worry as to why the ongoing donor search had failed to turn up even a partial match for JoAnne diminished with each passing month. JoAnne was, after all, beating the odds, holding the disease at bay far beyond any of Dr. Gootenberg's predictions.

When summer turned to fall, JoAnne tackled a computer-science course at Georgetown. Perhaps, she told herself, she'd be able to return to Brown in January, despite what Dr. Gootenberg had said.

And then, as suddenly as it had come, the disease returned.

Through the chatter on the pediatric ward, JoAnne's mother over-heard two terrifying words whispered by a nurse into the telephone: "Two blasts."

Sylvia froze. "Are you talking about JoAnne?" she asked.

The nurse nodded, but explained that the test was inconclusive — abnormal but not leukemic. However, it was only a matter of time, Sylvia knew, before these "blasts" would spawn leukemic cells once again.

My daughter is going to die, she thought after Dr. Gootenberg's colleague, Dr. Lucius F. Sinks, confirmed in December 1989 that JoAnne had relapsed. That night she phoned her sister, Henrice Taylor, in Chicago. "If we don't find a donor for JoAnne, she will die," she said. "And if *we* don't find one, nobody will."

Over the next four days, Sylvia and Howard repeated those words to anyone in a position to make a difference. For years, the Johnsons had served on boards, worked on campaigns, volunteered their talents. Now they were the ones reaching out.

That Sunday, their living room was filled with people ready to help. The facts the Johnsons put before them were daunting. The doctors offered only the technology of transplantation, they explained to this newly formed committee. For the rest, they were on their own.

The federal government offered almost no financial assistance to families mounting private donor drives. It cost $75 to test one person. Just locating a match for JoAnne could cost more than $1 million. With her life measured in weeks, they would have to raise funds and test HLA types simultaneously.

JoAnne sat listening quietly as plans took shape for mailings, for a media blitz, for appeals to influential ministers. "What on earth do you call a campaign like this?" Sylvia wondered out loud.

For the first time all afternoon, JoAnne spoke. "Call it Save JoAnne," she said.

Armed with the breakdown of JoAnne's HLA type, Sylvia combed medical textbooks and journals and pieced out the frequencies with which JoAnne's antigens occurred among blacks — the population that the Johnsons intended to tap for the drive. Working on borrowed time, they were maximizing odds; it had long been known that HLA matches occur much more frequently within ethnic groups.

At home, Sylvia laid out the statistics for JoAnne, who was cramming for her computer-science final at Georgetown. JoAnne scanned the figures, then ran her long fingers over the buttons on her pocket calculator. In every other campaign she'd participated in, JoAnne had been the one out front. To have to sit by and watch someone else "Save JoAnne" tore at her. Now, suddenly, she was in the thick of things again, all energy and determination.

When the answer appeared on the calculator, she grinned at her mother. "One . . . in . . . eight . . . thousand!"

The figure was encouraging; they should have no trouble testing that many people in two months. But Sylvia was also puzzled. Among blacks, JoAnne's HLA type was relatively common. With over 70,000 donors registered in the United States, why hadn't a single match turned up?

When Sylvia Johnson learned the explanation from her sister Henrice, she sat holding the phone in stunned silence. Finally she spoke, her voice thick with anger and incredulity. "There are only 800 blacks in the registry? That can't be, Henrice. Eight *hundred?*"

Again and again, she repeated the number her sister had learned from a California family seeking a donor for a black leukemia victim. A month earlier, Henrice said, the family had accessed the ethnic breakdown of the National Registry donor pool and discovered that only 300 blacks were registered. In the past month, they had tested 500 more. The number explained why there had never been a successful transplant in a black patient.

"So it is 800 then," Sylvia said. She realized the search so far had been an empty exercise, given the poor odds of a black patient finding a match among white donors. Only now, with JoAnne in relapse, had the family learned her chances of locating a match had been close to zero all along.

"Close to zero until now," JoAnne responded when her mother reported the grim statistic. "We're going to be the ones to change it from 800 to 8000."

The look on JoAnne's face was one her mother had seen before. It was a winner's look, a look that brooked no argument.

From the moment the first Save JoAnne fliers hit the mail, the Johnsons refused to take no for an answer. "With or without you, we are going forward," Howard told Dr. Gootenberg when he counseled against embarking on a $1 million drive against such long odds.

"You are only one family," Dr. Gootenberg told them. Then, sensing the family's resolve, he shook his head. "You'll be out there alone. We'll help you as much as we can, but we're new to this too. The technology is just unfolding, and the registry isn't ready for it. We had no more idea than you did of the situation with minority donors. Look at the odds against you. As JoAnne's doctor, I feel your time would be better spent with JoAnne."

Howard looked at his wife, and then at Dr. Gootenberg. "If you're trying to dissuade us, you are wasting your time," he said.

Henrice, meanwhile, was learning what it meant to be, as Dr. Gootenberg put it, "out there alone." But, like her sister and brother-in-law, she was undaunted.

"If you just come out and get tested, I'll owe you my life."

Naysayers fell by the wayside as the urgency of the Save JoAnne campaign took hold. The most influential ministers in Chicago and Washington offered their churches as testing sites. Washington newspapers ran stories about the donor drive. Chicago radio stations scheduled Susan Fundukian, Henrice's business partner, for a Christmas Day appeal, while Washington news anchor Paul Berry booked JoAnne and her mother for his December 28 show.

When Henrice arrived to celebrate Christmas, the hastily organized committee had already locked up three testing drives, to begin December 28. Every detail of the Save JoAnne campaign was meticulously in place —except for JoAnne's leukemia cells. Instead of retreating under the bombardment of drugs, as they had before, they were multiplying.

"There's no point in continuing the chemotherapy. It is not working," Dr. Sinks told the family two days after Christmas. Just as Dr. Gootenberg had predicted a year before, the toughest cells had gone into hiding and undergone a process called clonal evolution. Now, in their more advanced mutation, they were impervious to every drug in the oncologists' arsenal.

Gone was the three- or four-month remission the Johnsons had hoped to buy for JoAnne. Even if a preliminary match turned up by the end of January, final-stage testing could take weeks.

Henrice Taylor's experience told her that the measured campaign they'd planned would not be enough. "When your child is dying and you have no time, you just start begging," she urged Sylvia after she balked at the no-holds-barred approach.

"People will understand that this is urgent. I know how to recruit, and I can beg harder and step on more toes than you can, because I don't live here!"

Won over by Henrice's conviction, Sylvia and Howard handed her the reins. She canceled her flight home, delegated the Chicago drive to Fundukian, and spent the next 20 hours on the telephone. By the following morning, the Johnsons' home resembled a political-campaign office. Charts and calendars covered the walls. Newly installed 800 lines crisscrossed the family room. Calls to the Johnsons' neighbors, friends, colleagues, as well as to local hospitals, had paid off: a tiny army of volunteers stood ready to man the home office and staff four testing sites for a New Year's Eve drive.

But no one could beg, buy or guarantee the donors. No one, including Henrice, knew whether it was really possible to draw people out on New Year's Eve to have their blood tested for a 19-year-old girl they'd never met.

Channel Seven broadcast the pleas, one by one, on December 28: first, Paul Berry called on viewers to rally; Dr. Clive Callender of Howard University Hospital urged the black community to mobilize; Sylvia Johnson, head down, softly explained how simple and painless the HLA test was. "It takes less time than parking your car," she said.

JoAnne spoke last. "I'm pleading to people," she said, looking straight into the camera. "This is my life, and without your help, I can't make it. I know my match is out there. If you just come out and get tested, I'll owe you my life."

Some 1300 people lined up in the icy drizzle on New Year's Eve, spilling onto the street outside Grace Lutheran and Metropolitan A.M.E. churches. Inside, people rolled up their sleeves and donated the two tablespoons of blood needed for HLA typing.

"What you've undertaken is incredible. There must be some way I can help," a young man named Tom Smith told Howard Johnson. An hour later Smith was sitting in the Johnsons' family room, amid a crowd of volunteers and tangle of phone lines, helping Henrice set up a computer record-keeping system for the drive.

It was clear they were going to need it. Every call brought unexpected offers of help.

"My little girl had leukemia. Thank God, she survived, but I know what you're going through," a professor at the University of the District of Columbia told Henrice. "I want to help you set up a drive at U.D.C."

Calls came from JoAnne's schoolmates, from a childhood friend of her mother's, from total strangers who had seen JoAnne on television. Everybody in Washington wanted to do something. The lines of people standing under umbrellas in the icy rain kept growing longer. Henrice phoned Howard University Hospital to recruit more phlebotomists to draw blood. Long lines almost always meant lost volunteers, and they could not afford to lose a single sample. But no one left. By 6 p.m., there were three times as many donors as there were testing kits. The chances of reaching the supplier on New Year's Eve seemed slim, but Henrice figured she had to try.

"Slow down, JoAnne," they pleaded. "Nope, gotta keep going. . ."

She repeated her request to four Roche Biomedical Laboratories supervisors before she reached the company's lab manager at his home: "I hope you can help me, sir. My niece is dying, and I stand to lose hundreds of blood samples."

Taylor got what she needed: a shipment of the lab's remaining testing kits, and a crew to open the lab on New Year's Day.

Her hands were shaking as she hung up the phone at 10:10. Her niece had tapped a well of empathy she hadn't known existed. If testing at the other sites was going half as well, they'd have more than 1000 samples in one night. Perhaps JoAnne's match was already in, somewhere among the blood samples packed in the vans heading for Roche labs. If not, she had another media blitz and four mass screenings scheduled for next weekend.

JoAnne's voice broke into her thoughts. "Henrice, I'm having chills. Could someone please take my temperature?"

Her flushed face bespoke the onset of a fever even before the thermometer confirmed her 102-degree temperature. Fever, the sign of infection, was especially dangerous in an immunosuppressed patient.

"I want her here within the hour," Dr. Gootenberg told Henrice when she reached him on the ward.

It wasn't until the next morning, when she read the Washington *Post* in her hospital room, that JoAnne understood what had happened the night before. It might just be more powerful than the leukemia that had tried to derail her life at every turn.

The *Post* told of volunteers standing in line in the cold rain, each one convinced he or she would be JoAnne's match. With her simple request for a shot at life, she had doubled the number of blacks in the National Registry, overnight.

In the scramble for supplies on New Year's Eve, Henrice had come face to face with an unpleasant reality: the HLA typing system was set up for a slow, measured influx of donors. Determined not to fall victim to her own success, Henrice searched for ways to circumvent the system's limitations. They could not afford to lose a single sample.

Already, in the first wave of donors, partial matches had been identified at several times the frequency in the existing registry. The odds of locating a perfect match among black donors looked excellent —but whether that would happen before JoAnne's strength failed, no one could be certain.

Perhaps, Sylvia suggested, less-than-perfect would have to do. It was possible, she had learned, to achieve a successful graft with a partial HLA match. But the risks were so great that the few medical centers to attempt the operation— Georgetown not among them—set high physical standards for admission. Even with a perfect match, the transplant procedure was difficult, involving massive chemotherapy and total body irradiation to kill the diseased marrow. For a partial match, the patient's heart and lungs must be strong enough to withstand the rejection phenomena that inevitably followed.

JoAnne prepared herself for the cardiopulmonary tests ahead of her with an athlete's single-mindedness. When her match came in, she told the oncology team, she intended to be ready. The nurses, for whom "walking a patient" usually meant pushing a wheelchair, found themselves jogging behind JoAnne as she did laps around the hospital courtyard, her portable I.V. pole rattling across the concrete.

"Slow down, JoAnne, slow down!" they pleaded, worried lest she go into cardiac arrest.

"Nope, gotta keep going," JoAnne called over her shoulder. Bundled up against the damp cold of Washington winter, she pushed to finish her self-imposed half-mile regimen.

Henrice, meanwhile, was pushing the blood-typing system to its limits. Learning that the National Registry's recruitment staff and lab network could not accommodate her needs, she was forced to regroup quickly. While 700 volunteers stood in line, waiting to be tested, she plunged into the labyrinth of independent labs and competing donor registries.

In a series of frantic phone calls, she managed to enlist the aid of the American Registry, a smaller national network able to aid family recruitment drives. But that was only half the battle. The network of approved testing labs, inundated that weekend by similar drives across the country, was collapsing under the load. By the time Henrice learned of Genetic Design — certified lab that did HLA typing and could handle a large volume — she had lost hours.

Seven hundred potential donors, assuming the drive had ended during the delay, left. The Johnsons would never know whether JoAnne's match might have been among them. But the tiny army of volunteers refused to be undone.

Tom Smith and JoAnne's brother Stephen, braving an ice storm that had hit Washington that day, shuttled testing kits from Howard and

Georgetown hospitals to the recruiting sites. By night's end, a cadre of volunteers had logged in 1500 more samples.

JoAnne's hope lay in those samples, and in the startling results of her cardiopulmonary tests. Once again, she had defied the odds: after a year of chemotherapy, it seemed she had retained enough strength to withstand a transplant operation.

The preliminary results of the HLA typing came closer than any before: one near match was identified from the first group of donors, and then, a few days later, a second. As JoAnne and her parents conferred with Dr. Gootenberg and agonized over their options, a call from the University of Kentucky Medical Center tipped the scale. Kentucky was willing to consider JoAnne for a mismatched transplant with a family member.

JoAnne closed her eyes and leaned back when she was told the news from Kentucky. A tired version of her I-told-you-so grin spread slowly over her face.

"Your timing's perfect, JoAnne," exulted Natasha Rabchevsky, who hoped to land a summer job at the French Embassy, next door to Georgetown Hospital. "I could walk across the courtyard and visit you every day—only this time, instead of getting sicker, you'll be getting better and better."

It was not to be. JoAnne's previous cardiac output tests hadn't told the whole truth, the Johnsons learned when they arrived at Kentucky's transplant center. Or, to be more precise, they had accurately recorded JoAnne's cardiac output at particular moments the week before. JoAnne knew, as no one else did, that those moments represented the very edge of her endurance.

The truth, on January 13, 1990, when JoAnne was retested at Kentucky, was that she had little chance of surviving a transplant operation. More than the lab results, the huge, open sores in her mouth and esophagus—the results of chemotherapy—betokened a ravaged immune system.

"You mean there's nothing to be done? You have nothing to offer us?" Howard asked. The doctors in Kentucky shook their heads.

Overwhelmed, JoAnne's father held her close. "I don't know why God has chosen you for this," he said.

"Neither do I, Daddy," JoAnne told him. "I love you and Mom more than anything in the world. I want you both to know that. As long as I'm alive, there'll be something to do. There's *always* something to do."

Back in her room at Georgetown, isolated from contamination by a glass anteroom, JoAnne bore down on the task she'd set for herself. She had a simple problem before her: mouth sores.

Her keyboard and her jazz tapes sat idle. Except for the Bible, her books were set aside. Methodically, JoAnne applied the ointments to her mouth, never deviating from her regimen, never forgetting that her match might be among the next wave of volunteers.

The numbers of donors did not slacken. Person after person, waiting in line, insisted that he would be the one. JoAnne's quiet plea had turned Washington upside down. In the Johnsons' family room the noise was deafening as phones rang around the clock with offers of help.

In her room, where the only sound was the occasional bleep of her I.V., JoAnne began to draw. She drew cells, exquisitely intact on one page, exploding into chaos on the next. Over and over, she willed the destruction of the voracious, twisted cells of her leukemia.

And then, intrigued by picture books that a counselor was assembling for the youngest patients, JoAnne offered her help. "I've drawn enough for myself. I want to draw for other people," she told the counselor, and turned her pen once again to clowns and rainbows.

JoAnne never stopped walking—though each day, as she fought back the exhaustion of her latest drug treatment, her walks grew shorter. She slept, woke, listened hungrily to news of the donor drive, and visited with the people she loved.

With her grandmother, Katie Taylor-Moore, affectionately known as "Kay-Kay," JoAnne reminisced about the family's summer visits. She remembered how, sitting on the front porch of the big frame house, they'd talked by the hour. JoAnne revealed her plans to be a "brain surgeon, a professor, an actress and a mother with ten kids."

That evening she waited eagerly, as she did every evening, for her parents' arrival, and news of the drive. It was always the same—nothing yet, but soon, very soon.

When the campaign she'd named Save JoAnne just eight weeks earlier broke the 5000 mark in early February, JoAnne dreamed that her match had been found. The vividness of the dream shot her bolt upright in bed. "Did you say they found it? The perfect match?" she asked the nurses.

"No, JoAnne," the nurse told her gently.

"But I heard you," JoAnne insisted. "I just heard you say they'd found my match."

"I'm sorry, JoAnne. I wish I had said that. But I didn't. You must have been dreaming."

JoAnne fell back to sleep, too tired to argue.

At last, she was simply too tired — too tired to survive a transplant when on February 9 a near match was found; too tired to understand her family's agony in recognizing, on February 16, that there was nothing left but to have done with the machines and the sterile room, and take JoAnne home.

When JoAnne dreamed again, it was of heaven, she confided to a friend, "and what it would be like."

A thousand people rose to their feet, singing, rocking Grace Lutheran Church with music on February 23, the day of JoAnne Johnson's funeral.

Together, against all odds, they had done it.

237

"We have to find a way to use what happened to me," JoAnne had told visitor after visitor in the last days of her life—and her family had done it, setting up the JoAnne Katherine Johnson Foundation to help other families. And they refused to stop the marrow drive even when it was no longer possible to save JoAnne, showing up at a local college to test volunteers the day after her death. Already, the total number of black marrow donors had increased eightfold.

That legacy resounded in every chord of JoAnne's beloved music, played by her high-school jazz ensemble. But it was in the subtlety of her own pen strokes that she spoke most eloquently, in the drawing reproduced on the funeral program cover.

"Window of Hope," she called her final sketch, an unfinished pen-and-ink rendition of a leafless tree, done from her sickbed one late autumn day. Delicate, its outer edges only dimly penciled in, it celebrated the unyielding optimism of JoAnne and of her family, who had vowed to "turn the world upside down." Together, against all odds, they had done it—and forever changed the world for other children.

The pony-tailed ten-year-old who knocked shyly at the door of her guidance counselor's office knew nothing of JoAnne Johnson and the family in Washington that had just "turned the world upside down." Katrina Whetstone's life in the town of Chester, S.C., had been in a state of chaos ever since she had learned, in the summer of 1988, that she had leukemia.

"Can I come in, Mrs. Wylie?" she asked.

Counselor Linda Wylie looked at the chubby face full of something far beyond ordinary fifth-grade troubles, and motioned Katrina in.

"Mrs. Wylie, I'm scared I'm going to die," Katrina blurted out.

Linda Wylie was speechless. Katrina, with her sparkling eyes and plump cheeks, looked as healthy as any child she'd ever seen.

"The doctor said I had three years before I'd get really sick," Katrina began. Slowly at first, then rapidly, she told the counselor about leukemia, about how it hid and lay in wait and then killed you. Katrina catalogued the names of the drugs she was taking, and talked about her friends from Camp Kemo, the summer camp for children with cancer.

Katrina explained that the doctors were searching for someone whose tissue type matched hers, so she could have a bone-marrow transplant. But the search for the matching donor was hard to understand.

Katrina looked at her counselor and asked a question she didn't really want answered: "Mrs. Wylie, what if they don't find a match for me in time?"

Three thousand miles away, at the Fred Hutchinson Cancer Research Center in Seattle, the woman assigned to find that match had been asking herself the same question for two years. She was looking for the same needle in a haystack that had eluded JoAnne Johnson. And so far, it eluded her too.

She studied the computer printout and the rows of zeros. Two lined up under the letter A, two under B—codes for the first of the six antigens that must be matched before the others could be checked for compatibility. Second-stage testing, of the so-called DR antigens, came later, out of the group of people identified as AB matches. But the zeros that lined up with chilling predictability month in, month out, indicated this search was not going to get that far.

Every eight weeks a letter went out to Katrina's physician, Dr. Ronnie Neuberg, and another to her parents, Carolyn and James Whetstone. Every letter was the same: "We are sorry to report that no potential donors have been identified. We will continue to search and will notify you of any developments."

When the letters arrived, Katrina's mother slit them open, read them and tucked them in her dresser drawer. *When good news comes, we'll tell Katrina,* she thought. *Why should a ten-year-old have to carry around that kind of worry?*

But one January night Carolyn Whetstone learned that Katrina understood how grim her outlook was. Carolyn was cleaning up after dinner, when Katrina's voice cut through the clatter of dishes. "I'm not afraid to die, Mama," she said. Katrina had been watching a television special on children with cancer. "Those kids on the show were all afraid.

But I'm not like them. I know if I die, I'll go to heaven. So I'm not afraid."

The queasiness that Carolyn had lived with for two years tightened into a hard knot in her stomach. "That's my brave girl," she said. "Don't be afraid. But don't stop hoping, either. And don't stop praying. I'll be praying for you tonight."

For two years, Carolyn had prayed her way through her midnight-to-eight shift at the Springs Mills textile factory. More than once she'd looked up from her post on the line to see co-workers staring at her. Embarrassed, she riveted her eyes on the huge bobbin spinning before her and pressed her lips together. But she never stopped praying. *So many people care about Katrina,* she told herself. *I can't give up.*

She thought of her husband's personnel manager, Ray Smith, who, after learning of Katrina's situation two years ago, had gone straight to his boss at Sequa Chemicals, Inc. In a few days, James Whetstone had a promise. He would not have to worry about money. Ray Smith had told him: "You and Carolyn take care of Katrina. We'll take care of the rest."

But money alone couldn't save Katrina. A donor had to be found—and soon. So Carolyn kept praying. In one part of her mind she repeated the same words, over and over, no matter what else she was doing: Please, Lord, don't let her die.

Hope was only the beginning of what JoAnne Johnson had helped to create.

When things began to happen, it was so sudden, so unexpected, that at first Lauri Gill, Katrina's new search coordinator, assumed that the report was wrong. Where the zeros had been, there were now numbers —row after row of numbers!

There was no mistake. After two years of nothing, the system had just identified four AB matches for Katrina Whetstone.

It was as though they had come out of nowhere, Gill thought. She did not know about the Save JoAnne campaign and the groundswell it had created, as other black families took up the cause. All over the country, black leukemia patients were finding new hope in the sudden influx of thousands of African-American donors. Still, to match a donor involved two more levels of testing and an actual mixing of patient and donor blood. Although she was hopeful, all of Gill's experience taught her it was best to proceed with caution.

But caution was not what people in Chester wanted to hear. "Start the DR typing immediately, and let us know if you need more money," Ray Smith told Lauri Gill by phone. "It sure sounds hopeful to me."

The prayers that had begun in Carolyn's church soon echoed in every church in Chester County. Now there was something specific to ask for —that one of the four "possibles" would be the one for Katrina.

The news hit with a dull thud. None of the four, the Hutchinson Center reported, had proved compatible at the DR level.

"I feel like we're right back where we started," Carolyn told Ray Smith.

"No you're not. If they found four, they'll find four more. I've got a feeling about this."

In fact, though Smith and the Whetstones did not know it, the explosion in the pool of black donors that had changed the zeros to numbers—and hope—was only the beginning of what JoAnne Johnson had helped create.

As Lauri Gill re-entered a search request for Katrina, JoAnne Johnson's story was being told in the halls of Congress. JoAnne's face, her voice and, finally, her death, had set off waves of sympathy.

While Chester waited and prayed, the Sequa Chemicals company funded tissue typing for 72 of its employees in the hope of finding Katrina a match. Congress, anticipating a need for bone-marrow transplants in the wake of the Gulf War, reallocated $4.5 million for tissue typing. Another $1.5 million enabled the National Marrow Donor Program to open a recruiting office in Chicago, headed by JoAnne's aunt Henrice, who for 18 months worked on increasing minority enrollment in the donor program.

Within six months of JoAnne's death, the pool of black donors hit the 16,000 mark. By the fall of 1991, it had reached 23,000. At that time, the growing group of donors had produced some half-dozen matches for black leukemia patients.

At the Hutchinson Center, more zeros changed to numbers for Katrina Whetstone. Another letter went out. Katrina jumped rope and raced her bike through the streets of Chester.

"I might be going to Seattle soon," she confided to her teacher, as the school year drew to a close. "I mean, if they find a match for me. When I have my operation, I'll have to stay out of school for a year. But then I'll be all better, for good."

"Katrina, that's wonderful," her teacher said. "I'm going to say a prayer that it will happen soon."

Katrina was tired, and her mother was worried when, on the afternoon of June 13, they drove to see Dr. Neuberg. "Mama, my chest feels heavy," Katrina complained, resting her head on the seat back.

As Dr. Neuberg listened to Katrina's breathing, then studied her X rays, he confirmed that she had pneumonia.

"It's a mild case," Dr. Neuberg told them, tearing off a prescription sheet. "Nothing to be too concerned about, provided we get her on antibiotics right away."

In the outer office, mother and daughter waited for the prescription to be filled. Dr. Neuberg appeared in the doorway a few moments later. He closed the consulting-room door and turned to Katrina and her mother.

"I just got a call from Seattle. They have found a match for Katrina." He paused, and broke into a huge smile. "All eight of this donor's antigens and sub-antigens match Katrina's. This is as close to perfect as you can get."

Carolyn Whetstone laughed, and then she began to cry. Katrina grinned at the spectacle of her softspoken, ladylike mother hugging "Dr. Ron" and blowing her nose.

Three years of terror evaporated. Then came wave after wave of disbelief—at the jubilation of the people of Chester, at the speed with which their insurance company swung into action to get them to Seattle and settled in an apartment for the four-month treatment.

People the family barely knew stopped them on the street to celebrate the news. But it was the person they'd never met, or seen, who seemed most incredible. Somewhere out there a person who knew nothing about Katrina except the fact of her leukemia was checking into a hospital and donating the marrow to make her well.

Three pints of healthy bone marrow arrived at Katrina's bedside at 6 p.m. on August 27, 1991, the day after final radiation treatment had destroyed her own marrow. Her time had been shorter than anyone realized; Katrina's blood tests, on admission to Hutchinson, revealed the return of the dreaded "blast" cells.

Vulnerable to every germ in the wake of the radiation, Katrina lay behind plastic curtains, watching Lauri Gill hand the nurse the cooler containing the marrow that, just 12 hours earlier, had been removed by needle and syringe from her donor.

Somewhere in the United States —Katrina and her parents had no idea where — the 36-year-old black woman who had donated the marrow was preparing to check out of the hospital, with only a slight backache and a bandage to remind her of the extraction procedure. If all went well one month later, her marrow would "become" Katrina's. Exactly 100 days later, Katrina boarded the plane for her trip home.

Even before the plane touched down in Charlotte, the public celebration of Katrina's historic operation had begun. Reporters, cameramen and Red Cross representatives crowded at the gate as Katrina and her family walked into the video lights on December 7, 1991.

The best part of being home, Katrina told the reporters, "is seeing my family again." Carolyn, sitting behind her daughter at the press conference arranged by the Charlotte Red Cross, grinned at the understatement.

As the countdown to Christmas began, Katrina's blood tests at Children's Hospital in Columbia confirmed what the doctors at the Hutchinson Center had said: she was free of cancer. *That* was her Christmas present, Carolyn told the family when her brothers and sisters and their children gathered at her mother's for a noisy Christmas Eve celebration in Chester.

The stack of letters filled with bad news sat in Carolyn Whetstone's dresser drawer, beneath a handwritten note on lined steno paper. It was the note that she'd been handed the night the marrow had arrived, from the stranger who had changed everything.

"I feel very blessed to be able to do this for you," the woman had written. "I knew from the first pinch of blood that any life-giving effort on my part would come without hesitation. I thank God and Jesus Christ; and quoting from a part of Scripture from Romans: 'So as much as is in me, I am ready . . .'"

"I feel very blessed to able to do this for you."

244

ACKNOWLEDGMENTS

All the stories in *Windows of Hope* previously appeared in Reader's Digest Magazine. We would like to thank the following contributors and publishers for permission to reprint material.

"SOLD! To the Young Man in Shorts" by Paul Harvey. © 1987 by Los Angeles Times Syndicate, Gastonia Gazette (July 21, '87).

Monday Morning Miracle by Pattie Wigand as told to Philip Yancey. © 1988 by Philip Yancey, Family Circle (February 23, '88).

Room at the Table by James DiBello. "The Angel Who Saved My Marriage" from "TOUCHED BY ANGELS," edited and copyright © 1993 by Eileen Freeman. Reprinted by permission of Warner Books, Inc.

The Cellist of Sarajevo by Paul Sullivan. © 1996 by Paul Sullivan. Hope (March/April '96).

Life's Extras by Archibald Rutledge. "PEACE IN THE HEART," copyright © 1927, renewed 1957 by Archibald Rutledge. Originally published by Doubleday, a division of Random House, Inc.

A Prisoner's Tale by Everett Alvarez, Jr., and Anthony S. Pitch. "CHAINED EAGLE," copyright © 1989 by Everett Alvarez, Jr., and Anthony S. Pitch. Originally published by Donald I. Fine, Inc.

Lusin, from "THE WISDOM OF CHINA AND INDIA," edited by
   Lin Yutang (Random House).
Albert Einstein, "IDEAS AND OPINIONS" (Crown Publishers).
Marilyn Thomsen in Signs of the Times (May '93).
Biblical scriptures are from the "REVISED STANDARD VERSION
   OF THE BIBLE," National Council of the Churches of Christ in the
   USA (Thomas Nelson)

Photo credits:

Cover landscape photo by Sven Halling/Panoramic Images
Title page photo by Darrell Gulin/Tony Stone Images
p. 6: Mary Rozzi/Graphistock
p. 11: Index Stock Photography
p. 16: Garry Black/Masterfile
p. 21: Kamil Vojnar/photonica
p. 23: Jana León/Graphistock
p. 26: Bruce Forster/Tony Stone Images
p. 28: Alan L. Detrick/Photo Researchers, Inc.
p. 33: Paul Grebliunas/Tony Stone Images
p. 41: Tim Brown/Tony Stone Images
p. 48: Gilbert S. Grant/Photo Researchers, Inc.
p. 55: Martin Rogers/Tony Stone Images
p. 58: Jim Steinberg/Photo Researchers, Inc.
p. 65: Susie Cushner/Graphistock
p. 68: Masao Ota/photonica
p. 81: Tim Hazael/Tony Stone Images
p. 82-83: Vaughan Fleming/Science Photo Library, Photo Researchers
p. 89: Index Stock Imagery
p. 97: Phil Schermeister/Tony Stone Images
p. 107: Mark Tomalty/Masterfile

p. 116: Bob Winsett/Index Stock Photography, Inc.

p. 124: Robert A. Isaacs/Photo Researchers, Inc.

p. 130: Joyce Photographics/Photo Researchers, Inc.

p. 139: Allan Davey/Masterfile

p. 149: David Zaitz/photonica

p. 162: Rafael Macia/Photo Researchers, Inc.

p. 169: Adam Jones/Photo Researchers, Inc.

p. 175: Dennis O'Clair/Tony Stone Images

p. 184: Index Stock Photography, Inc.

p. 191: Kevin Leigh/Index Stock Phography, Inc.

p. 196: Chip Henderson/Tony Stone Images

p. 203: Index Stock Imagery

p. 208: Kathryn Szoka/Graphistock

p. 210: Nick Vaccaro/photonica

p. 212: Landscape photo by Sven Halling/Panoramic Images

Carousel Research: Laurie Platt Winfrey, Van Bucher